D1360736

**Engineering a New Architecture**

# Engineering

# a

# New

# Architecture

Tony Robbin

*Foreword by Stuart Wrede*

Yale University Press
New Haven and London

*Frontispiece:* The Hajj Terminal at the King Abdulaziz International Airport in Saudi Arabia (fig. 2.6).

Designed by James J. Johnson and set in Aster Roman types by Highwood Typographic Services, Hamden, Connecticut.
Printed in the United States of America by Quebecor-Eusey Press, Leominster, Massachusetts.

*Library of Congress Cataloging-in-Publication Data*
Robbin, Tony.
    Engineering a new architecture / Tony Robbin : foreword by Stuart Wrede.
      p.  cm.
    Includes bibliographical references and index.
    ISBN 0-300-06116-1 (cloth : alk. paper)
    1. Structural design. 2. Geodesic domes. 3. Shells (Engineering).
    I. Title
    TA658.2.R63   1996
    624.1'771—dc20                   95-36222

A catalogue record for this book is available from the British Library.

The paper in this book meets the guidelines for permanence and durability of the Committee on Production Guidelines for Book Longevity of the Council on Library Resources.

10  9  8  7  6  5  4  3  2  1

**To Horst Berger,**
**for his great contribution to**
**membrane structures**

# Contents

# Foreword

A fundamental tenet of the modern movement in architecture was that structure, material, and technique determined form; new materials and structural systems, as they evolved, gave shape to the architecture of their time. Structures built with advanced engineering techniques—long-span bridges, exposition buildings, factories, and great glass-and-steel railway stations—became important prototypes, and glass, steel, and concrete the modern materials par excellence. The engineer emerged as an important role model for the architect.

As early as the 1920s the avant-garde architects in Russia proposed daring structures in these new materials, but the construction industry, particularly in the still largely agrarian Soviet Union, was not capable of realizing them. A renewed post–World War II enthusiasm, both for modernism and for advanced structures, led to such experimental work as Matthew Nowicki's State Fair Arena in Raleigh, North Carolina; the Yale hockey rink and the TWA and Dulles airport terminals by Eero Saarinen; and the Sidney Opera House by Jørn Utzon. Engineer designers like Buckminster Fuller and Frei Otto became heroes in the profession. But much of this innovative work had significant limitations in terms of the maturity of the technology and (in the case of the Sidney Opera House) its costs. Materials, while improving rapidly, were not always up to requirements.

But it was a wider disillusionment with the modern movement that caused architects' interest to shift radically. The profession is notoriously fickle in its enthusiasms; still, the shift was justified. As modern architecture became the dominant mode of building in the postwar years, the reality of the results differed sharply from the ideal. The seemingly laudable concern for affordability, function, and efficiency too often generated buildings that were diagrammatic, shabbily built, and of little artistic merit. Particularly in urban planning, it became increasingly apparent, too, that the ideal was highly flawed. The city environment became ever more inhuman and alienating as traditional centers were torn apart in the name of progress and urban renewal.

Although the critique of the modern movement was sound, the reaction in the profession, when it finally came, missed the mark: architects embraced an often clumsy and facile historical eclecticism. In this climate, advanced engineering structures were forgotten.

But while architects were enthusiastically admiring their past and doing research on everyone from Michelangelo to Addison Mizner, a number of engineers quietly developed and refined the innovations in structures and materials that Fuller, Otto, and other pioneers had made in the postwar years. As Tony Robbin admirably documents in this book, enormous progress has been made. Methods and materials

have matured, new concepts and systems have
emerged, and many remarkable structures have
been built. It is past time for architects to once
again pay attention, and marvel, and, one hopes,
be less naively optimistic about the ability of
technology to solve all problems. In fact—a
promising sign—a new generation of architects
is again drawing inspiration from this work.

It is indicative that the writer of this book is
not an architect but an artist who has himself
done pioneering work on four-dimensional structures. He brings to the book a fresh eye and a
sense of the structures' great beauty. One can
only hope that those in the profession will stop
looking mainly in the rearview mirror for inspiration or engaging in increasingly esoteric
debate. When new histories of architecture are
written, the buildings in this book may seem
considerably more significant than the eclectic
pastiches and the deconstructed piles that now
command most of the attention.

STUART WREDE

# Acknowledgments

In this book I emphasize the contributions of engineers, even though the efforts of architects and contractors are also needed to build the new structures that I write about. I have tried to mention architects and contractors in all cases, but if their contributions seem to be slighted, I hope to be forgiven on the grounds that usually it is the other way around: the contributions of engineers are slighted.

I wish to thank Ron Check and Mat Levy for access to the Weidlinger Associates library, without which the research for this book would have been impossible; David Campbell, Stanley Hallet, Haresh Lalvani, Charles Peck, Bill Perk, and Ron Shaeffer for special photos and access to their personal libraries; Elizabeth Weatherford for her consultation on the tipi; and Clara Van Beek for her translation of Mick Eekhout's Dutch writing. All of the engineers mentioned in the book have been wonderful about sending photographs, and I am grateful.

To Ture Wester, who brought me into the International Association for Shell and Space Structures, and to my colleagues in the Structural Morphology Group a special thanks for making me feel welcome.

The readers of the manuscript for this book have given me valuable insights. I am indebted to Andrew Vernooy for his enthusiastic support, to René Motro for reviewing my discussion of tensegrity, and, in particular, to David Campbell for his careful scrutiny of my work. Stuart Wrede not only read early drafts and gave good counsel but provided a fine foreword; he has my gratitude.

Birdair, Inc., fabric roof contractor, enthusiastically supported this project, giving me many color photos as well as a travel grant to allow me to view more membrane structures in person. A grant from the Graham Foundation for Advanced Studies in the Fine Arts provided further support. I appreciate the faith that Judy Metro, senior editor at Yale University Press, has shown in me, as well as the careful contributions of Mary Pasti, manuscript editor. As always, this project would have been no fun without my agent, Robin Straus.

# Introduction

In a televised interview Frank Lloyd Wright defined modern architecture: it was not architecture made in the modern period but rather "organic" architecture made with tensile strength.[1] He called the new principle "tenuity" and illustrated it by lacing his fingers together to make a tenuous, flexible but strong connection, which he associated with a railway trestle bridge. Post and beam construction, in contrast, is stacked, fist over fist, with neither tensile strength nor unity. In the interview, Wright said that tenuity—based on the long-span capabilities of steel—compelled him to develop "open plan" architecture, a design concept that he considered his greatest artistic contribution.

Wright, the master designer, thus gave priority to engineering. An engineer as well as an architect (he left engineering school just three months short of his degree), Wright saw no essential conflict between engineering and architectural design; rather, he saw that the converse is true: new aesthetics are the inescapable consequence of new engineering techniques. Wright claimed that if the ancient Greeks had developed steel and glass, they would have made "modern" architecture back then. He expressed loathing for those who clung to an architectural style when there was no functional or structural reason to do so.

The engineering of the present is ripe with possibilities for innovative design. Membrane structures redefine the meaning of inside and outside. Tensegrity systems of cables and rods elegantly balance the tension and compression in materials that hold up buildings. The rationality and efficiency of deployable structures, made at one location or at ground level on site and then erected in one operation, add a new dimension to the aesthetic appreciation of architecture. Shells, hybrids, computer-driven morphology studies, and exotic new materials also enrich architects' choices.

The modernist principle of placing engineering at the forefront of design is bringing us structures of great beauty and practicality. But first, for another example of how discoveries in engineering are the source of original architecture, let us look back at the Crystal Palace, a product of the industrial revolution in England.

The Crystal Palace is, according to the architectural historian Folke T. Kihlstedt, as influential a building as the Pantheon, the Hagia Sophia, or Abbot Suger's Cathedral of Saint Denis. But most Victorians, he says, "saw the Crystal Palace not as architecture but as construction; to their eye it was styleless and lacked decoration." Its standardized machine-made parts appeared to leave no room for choices based on taste. The building was influential for its practicality alone; the design was considered useful for temporary structures. After all, it was built by Joseph Paxton, a mere gardener and builder of greenhouses and most certainly not a beaux-arts architect.[2] Only now can we see that its practicality was based on many impressive structural innovations—innovations that were powerful enough, and handled with enough sensitivity and faith in their value, to change taste and define a new aesthetics, one that still speaks to us today (fig. 1.1).

The Crystal Palace was enormous—the main hall alone was 1,848 by 408 feet (with ceilings that averaged 72 feet in height), and the whole structure covered 19 acres in total—yet the enclosure was designed, prototyped, manufactured, delivered, and erected in an astonishingly short seventeen weeks' time; it was fully ready for occupancy in thirty-nine weeks. Originally built in 1851 to house the first world fair, it was dismantled the following year, moved, and rebuilt. (Contemporaries of Paxton saw the potential for redeployment of its standardized parts and proposed new configurations, including a glass-walled skyscraper.) Within three years of its completion, Crystal Palaces appeared in Dublin, New York, and Munich; others were still being built decades later (plate 1).

Newspapers reported the cost of the Crystal Palace to have been about one penny per cubic foot (200,000 British pounds for 33 million cubic feet). One penny was the cost of cleaning a pair of boots, 15 pence the cost of inexpensive but clean lodgings and a hearty breakfast, and 30 pence to one pound the fee for entrance to the exhibition.[3] Although engineers today do not report or compare costs per cubic foot, it is interesting to do so for a contemporary equivalent of the Crystal Palace, the 27,182-square-foot greenhouse to be built for the Botanical Garden of the Taiwan National Museum of Natural Science

1.1. Joseph Paxton's Crystal Palace, built in Hyde Park, London, in 1851, is illustrated in a contemporary newspaper. In the accompanying article, the writer marvels at the dimensions of this "vast temple," whose "total cubic contents [are] 33,000,000 feet."

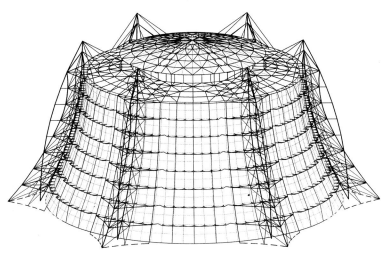

1.2. The greenhouse designed for the Botanical Garden at the Taiwan National Museum of Natural Science is similar to the original Crystal Palace. Also comparable, as it turns out, is the unit cost of construction. Bruce Danzinger, Ove Arup and Partners; Bryan Irwin and Ian Tyndall, architects. (Drawings courtesy Bruce Danzinger, Ove Arup and Partners.)

(fig. 1.2). The greenhouse will be a glass cylinder, supported by trusses and tension rods, with a volume of 2,750,000 cubic feet—about one-tenth the volume of the Crystal Palace. The estimated contract for the enclosure and foundation is $13,000,000 (U.S. dollars), giving a cost per cubic foot of $2.90, which we can translate using the previous purchasing-power yardsticks: $2.90 is top price for a boot polishing, but not if the services of a barber are included, as was the case in 1851; nor is $44.00 unreasonable for bed and breakfast at a motel; and a seat at the opera or a day at Disney World could easily cost $87.72. We have not made great progress in the cost-effectiveness of our large-span all-glass structures in the last 150 years.

For the Crystal Palace, the fast schedule and the mammoth size were accomplished by means of a remarkable array of structural innovations, from prestressing and glass curtain walls to ridge-and-furrow glass roofs and quick-assembly rigid frame connectors. *Prestressing* refers to the loading or bending of beams before they are placed in a structure, in order to augment their load-bearing capacity by canceling some of the expected load before it occurs. Paxton built 72-foot-long beams with a bend, or camber, of 10 inches, so that the beams would "sag" level when placed horizontally between columns: a prestressing by shape.[4] Additional prestress was provided by tie bars beneath the bottom edge (or chord) of the beam; these pure tension tie rods were made of wrought iron, which can have twice the tensile strength of cast iron. In general, the more easily made cast iron was used when structural members were in compression, as in pillars and short beams. Longer spans were trusses that looked thicker in the middle of the span when viewed from above or below but that looked straight and shallow when viewed from the side.

Sensitivity to the best structural use of materials and to the synergy of their combinations allowed Paxton to invent the emblem of modern architecture: the glass curtain wall. Strong post-and-beam construction, especially where the posts were cross-braced by pure tension tie rods, allowed for a redefinition of walls, from roof supports to thin skins that let in light and kept out weather. After the Crystal Palace was built, engineers soon realized that column supports

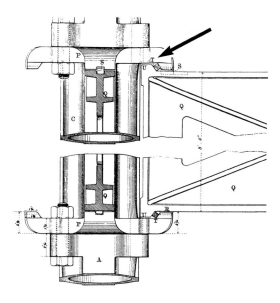

1.3. In the assembly system Paxton uses hammered keys, part T in his drawing, to speed-assemble portal frames.

could be moved inside the building, allowing the walls to be pure envelopes of glass.

Paxton also provided for a flat glass roof and a glass dome by using glass in a ridge and furrow configuration that "clearly anticipated" folded-plate or pleated construction, used today in reinforced concrete structures, where "the creased form adds stiffness."[5] Such a configuration in glass has the added advantage of being angled for maximum absorption and minimum reflection of morning and afternoon light, increasing natural light and heat.

Paxton would not have been able to build his giant glass house without the invention of a rigid connection node between metal posts and beams. (Rigid or bending-moment connections do not allow rotation at the joint and are the opposite of pin-connections, also called hinge connections, which allow free rotation at the joint.) Paxton's system of mass-produced, cast locking flanges, fixed in place by wrought-iron or oak keys hammered tight, provided for quick assembly and lateral stiffness (fig. 1.3). Indeed, every

corner where two beams and three posts met was a self-supporting component, which greatly reduced the need to erect scaffolding, which is expensive and time-consuming to put up.

Designing a building with the construction workers in mind was another of Paxton's concepts that we are only now beginning to appreciate. Cast parts were made so that workers had room to hammer in keys and use wrenches. Wooden sash bars and gutters were prepared and painted on the ground before being lifted to the roof. For the installation of the folded glass roof, there were traveling stages—mobile covered platforms—that ran along the roof gutters; loaded with a crew and materials, they "enabled 80 men to install 18,932 panes of glass in one week."[6] They also allowed the men to work in comfort and safety, in addition to increasing their productivity. The extensive use of power tools for drilling, hammering, hoisting, and even painting further augmented the workers' efforts.

Many of these technological innovations had precursors in early nineteenth-century techniques, but Paxton extended the techniques and put them together in an all-encompassing vision. Surely it is always like this: Separate technical innovations accrue, making our sense of space obsolete, although creator and viewer are aware only that vigor and freshness have somehow drained from their art and architecture. Then a great artist or innovator effectively redefines the very concept of space, giving it form and making our experience of it real to us. In architecture the process is not somehow to imbue construction with aesthetic value; rather, it is to redefine architectural space through the use of new engineering capabilities. We may enjoy the details and patterns of Victorian Crystal Palaces, even though contemporary viewers did not seem to consider the styling sufficiently charming or decorative, but far more important to us is that we can see how a building stands up, can read in the facade a diagram of the static forces of the structure. Once we know that a building can reveal its structure, buildings that do not, seem over-stuffed, murkily designed, and annoying. Paxton knew that his audience would be amazed at a vast open space defined by transparent surfaces and that they would be satisfied to know how the miracle came to pass. Indeed, this is what makes Crystal Palaces and their descendants beautiful to us, not the dated patterning on the facades.

As an introductory, hypothetical example of what is admirable in contemporary engineering, consider the advantages of a fabric structure over a conventional brick dome. (The comparison is extreme but allows me to make a rhetorical point.) Although bricks may be inexpensive to produce, in the aggregate they are heavy and laborious to lay; many bricks must be transported to the site and individually lifted into place. Once completed, the dome is dark inside, so either holes must be cut into it, which weakens the structure, or extra energy must be consumed in artificial light. Because bricks and mortar are not weathertight over time, an additional water shield (such as paint or copper cladding) must be applied and maintained, for should it fail and the mortar dissolve, the massive structure would be vulnerable to collapse. To expand or reconfigure a brick dome might require an extensive and dangerous demolition, with little opportunity to salvage materials or structure.

A fabric membrane structure is manufactured off site, assembled quickly on the ground, where it is safe and efficient to work, and then unfurled, or deployed, in one operation. Although erection can be complicated, the procedure does not require a scaffolding, which would greatly increase the cost while reducing safety and the accuracy of construction. Compared with hard structures in traditional materials, membrane structures are extremely lightweight, making them not only safer but also cheaper in many cases; a typical large-span membrane roof weighs one-fiftieth of a concrete dome.[7] Membranes are translucent yet fabricated to reflect most light waves, so they are both bright

and cool to use. Held together with just a few seams, they are especially weathertight and require little or no maintenance (see plate 17).

Teflon-coated fiberglass is expected to last at least thirty years—some say one hundred. With a shorter-lived membrane of polyester coated in polyvinyl chloride (PVC), inexpensive at an average $1.50 a square foot, it is economically feasible to replace the membrane as it wears out. On the other hand, many structures are obsolete in fifteen years, and occupants relocate, modify their structures, or just make do because the high cost of the initial construction has not been amortized. With membrane structures, occupants can reconfigure their buildings with minimal demolition and reconstruction expense. Also, membrane structures have low mass, are flexible, and can absorb shock and vibration—all of value in earthquake-prone areas. Thus, compared with a brick dome, a membrane dome is safer and quicker to construct, more weathertight, and cheaper to maintain, and in many cases it has a lower initial cost as well (plate 2).

The increased use of tension in materials capable of supporting great tensile forces can be seen as more conceptually elegant than employing older types of construction. Broadly speaking, each brick in a brick dome is held in place by compression (squeezed by every other brick), and the dome is prevented from buckling by the inherent stiffness of the bricks. Brick is stiff; it is strong in compression but weak in tension, having only $\frac{1}{50}$ the tensile strength of high-tensile steel.[8] Tensile structures have a primary advantage of not being subject to buckling failure and therefore not depending on the stiffness of materials but on their tensile strength. Here, great strength gains have been made, and greater gains are theoretically possible.

The University of Lancaster's Michael French has an interesting way to compare the tensile strength of material as a function of its weight by calculating the maximum length of a strand or bar of the material that could hang vertically from one attached end before it tears under its own weight. A typical strand of mild steel can be imagined to hang 2 miles without breaking; a new high-tensile-steel bridge strand could hang 12 miles. Teflon-coated fiberglass could hang 8 miles; a polyaramid (such as Kevlar) could hang 120 miles. Thus, new materials have made tremendous gains in tensile strength. It is inconceivable that similar gains can be made in materials' resistance to buckling.[9]

Compression structures are, furthermore, subject to "geometric" buckling, no matter how stiff the individual members. That is, only certain geometric shapes (such as the tetrahedron) are essentially rigid, whereas others (such as the cube) are not, and depend on the strength of rigid connections at the vertices. Tension structures are not subject to such large-scale geometric buckling.[10] Tensegrity structures that combine cables and struts are capable of exploiting these gains in material tensile strength. What was once a charming oddity is now a major engineering strategy.

For many engineers and architects, this engineering-centered conceptual elegance has become the basis for a new aesthetic, one based on the further fusion of structure and shelter; form, support, use, and mechanical systems are all integrated. Inside and outside are brought together by what is a membrane in the biological sense of being a permeable filter. The shapes of the membrane structures can be beautiful: graceful and intricate at the same time.

Many separate cultural forces, which we dare not arrogantly ignore, are propelling us toward new construction. As Z. S. Makowski has pointed out, the severe economic recession in much of the world in the past ten years has accelerated a natural desire for more efficient structures.[11] The increased speed with which technology and demographics change makes buildings obsolete quickly, further promoting the construction of buildings with low initial costs and redeployable spaces. The continuing evolu-

tion of democratic principles places a new value on worker safety and also encourages a respectful look at diverse vernacular architecture.

Also part of our culture is the promise of exquisitely strong materials from a revolution in materials science. Mario Salvadori, of Columbia University, has noted that steel is commonly produced with a tensile strength of 36,000 to 50,000 pounds per square inch, although strengths up to 300,000 pounds per square inch have been produced, and the theoretical maximum, based on the attraction of forces within steel crystals, is 4 million pounds.[12]

There is the even greater promise of "smart materials" to replace the usual brute-strength ones. These flexible, self-adjusting, even self-aware materials can be used in complex hybrid structural systems, where several structures are in the same place at the same time, each taking priority over the others as needed. These new architectural bones, skins, brains, and muscles combine to become a new organic engineering, to make buildings that have the adaptive strength of living systems.

Enhancing the possibilities for future structures is the recent wide use of computers, which allow for the development of extraordinarily complex building systems. Computers enable interactive design and analysis, giving designers immediate feedback on the structural qualities of prospective shapes. Computer programs are being written to find the optimal shapes for domes and membranes. The greatest value of computers may lie, however, in their ability to make visible the exotic geometric shapes that otherwise are intuited only by mathematicians who devote their lives to such studies. One school of thought in the engineering community holds that the new geometries generated by computers are the key to future structures. Not just mathematicians but computer scientists, physicists, and zoologists have information useful to "structural morphology" engineers, who specialize in the geometry of structures.

In the United States we think of engineers as second fiddles to maestro architects, as number-crunching, hands-on realists who only implement the dreams and ideas of trained aesthetes. Yet many engineers are visionaries and philosophers, though with responsibilities for the public safety that add enormous weight to their decisions. Sometimes, like Wright, they are both engineer and architect, breaking our prejudicial stereotype. In Japan architects and engineers even train together and do not specify a discipline until well into their studies.

An old joke says that if an architect builds a building without an engineer, it will fall down, but if an engineer builds a building without an architect, it will be demolished. This joke presents the classic American argument that architect and engineer complement each other's missing skills. Engineers sometimes do seem stuck on a boring minimalist aesthetic, ignoring the possibilities for visual complexity in dutiful obeisance to the god of efficiency. In spite of new engineer-ing materials and practices, architects sometimes do exasperatingly insist on doing things the hard way. But the thesis of this book is more radical, more fundamental, than the maxim in the old joke: I argue that tomorrow's aesthetic is implicit in today's engineering.

The fact is that architects need engineers for aesthetics as much as for structural calculations. There are no guarantees, of course, for there is no such thing as an automatic aesthetic, but the new vision, the new spirit of adventure, does seem to lie in new engineering practices. Like the Crystal Palaces of the nineteenth century, membrane structures, tensegrity structures, deployable structures, thin-shell structures, hybrid structures, and other new engineering-based structures will catch on because of their practicality, and will, unbeknownst to us, change our concept of beautiful architecture, as well as our sense of space. They are the hidden avant-garde in architectural design.

# Membranes

Since the 1960s, Frei Otto, Horst Berger, and David Geiger have championed the idea of using fabrics for architectural structures. Their unassailable argument is that only fabric membranes are truly lightweight, so only membranes are suited to spanning large areas. Membranes—inflated by air pumps, stretched over tent poles, or hung from exterior scaffolding—are desirable for their quick construction and disassembly, their translucence, and their startling appearance.

Resistance to using membranes in architecture is based on the assumption, now proved false, that a tent is not a building—that it is not strong, permanent, fireproof, or insulated. No more dramatic rebuttal of the first of these objections can be made than to show Horst Berger standing on roof of the Hajj Terminal in Saudi Arabia (fig. 2.1). In size and strength, his structure redefines the meaning of the word *tent;* an unarmed criminal would be hard put to escape from a membrane prison. In the United States there are now more than 250 large, permanent membrane structures, in cold climates as well as warm, delivered on schedule and on budget to their occupants, signed off by fire and building inspectors, and insured by companies not known to be cavalier with money. In short, they are buildings.

If only one individual were selected as responsible for the introduction of tensioned membrane structures into the architectural canon, the choice would be Horst Berger. In twenty-five years of practice, he has built forty membrane structures, including some of the first, biggest, and most beautiful. He is a committed teacher, a bench scientist, a hands-on model-maker, and one of the most respected engineers in the world. His works are true art because they move us to a new image of space as defined by buildings, and they will be influential far beyond their utilitarian value because they show us what rational buildings are supposed to be.

Berger speaks passionately about his philosophy of membrane structures, or "shape structures," as he sometimes calls them. Besides encompassing the practical and economic advantages of membranes, his philosophy offers rational, aesthetic, and even moral satisfaction. Equality and balance of structural elements, coherence and economy of means, congruence of architectural form and engineering structure, control of sun and shade, and the tuning of ambient sound—all these can be achieved by a membrane a few millimeters thick. Structures in which architecture and engineering are separated look arbitrary to his eye, whereas membranes not only unite shape and structure but do so—must do so—with graceful, complex curves. Only such doubly curved surfaces work for tensioned membranes, and the subtle, evocative curvature is beautiful to the contemporary eye.

With Berger's philosophy, we are moved to

2.1. Horst Berger standing on the Hajj Terminal roof. Skidmore, Owings, and Merrill, architect and engineer; Horst Berger, consulting engineer. (Photo courtesy Horst Berger.)

see beyond a simplistic dichotomy of inside and outside; instead, we see membranes as the surface of exchange, the filter that brings inside and outside together: membranes in a biological sense. As the architect Todd Dalland has also emphasized, membranes can let anything in (sunlight, heat, fresh air), keep anything out (ultraviolet light, cold, moisture), push anything out (noise, excess heat), and keep anything in (heat, sound, coolness, moisture).[1]

Finally, Berger says that when he was a student there were 2 billion people in the world; now there are twice that number, and when his students are his age, the total will be doubled again. "If we are to make it," he says, "we must soon accept an aesthetics of economy."[2] There is an imperative tone to Berger's discourse: we have no right to waste solar energy; engineering is

more than number crunching. It is important to keep these philosophical goals in mind when looking at the development of membrane structures.

According to Ron Shaeffer, professor of architecture at Florida A. & M. University, a tent is the "oldest dwelling except for the cave."[3] He reports that mammoth bones and tusks were used to support animal hides more than 40,000 years ago in Ukraine. By 2000 B.C.E. tents were in widespread use in Europe, Asia, North America, and Africa, and these were usually of the Kibitka or yurt type, their cylinder walls ending in a conical roof. In Mongolia yurts are deployed by first expanding a scissor mechanism, then bending the resulting thin plane into the walls of the tent.

The black tent, another type of tent, named for the dark goat's hair from which the mem-

2.2. The traditional Black Tent of Afghanistan provides shade and ventilation through the open-weave goat-hair fabric. (Photo: Stanley Ira Hallet and Rafi Samizay; see Hallet & Samizay 1980.)

brane is woven, is formed from a combination of interior poles and exterior tension cables staked into the ground. It is a marvelous example of membrane engineering. Used primarily in hot dry climates like those of the Middle East and northern Africa, its dark color provides shade and its loose weave permits hot air to escape, yet, when wet, the fibers mat to provide relief from rain (fig. 2.2).

The third basic type of tent is the tipi, whose sophisticated structural and climate control properties will be discussed in Chapter 6.

Shaeffer likes to remind his audiences that circus big tops were common in the United States until the 1950s, some of them covering an area 2.5 acres in size. He urges us to see membrane architecture as a continuation of an uninterrupted tradition, not a radical new departure.

Despite Shaeffer's suggestion, something dramatic happened in the history of membrane structures at the Osaka Expo in 1970. David Geiger's large inflated membrane structure for

the U.S. Pavilion "captured the imagination of all who saw it" (fig. 2.3; box).[4] Davis, Brody, Chermayeff, Geismar, and de Mark was the architect for the project. Inspired by Walter Bird's air-supported "radomes" (domes for use as radar domes) of the 1950s (fig. 2.4), the low-profile cable-restrained dome spanned an area 262 by 460 feet and weighed only 1.25 pounds per square foot; it cost $4.50 a square foot (an extremely low cost per square foot, even for that time). It had such a low profile that wind created only uplift; two typhoons at the pavilion site, with winds on the order of 90 miles per hour, caused no damage or deflation.

The success of this structure encouraged Geiger to search for a permanent, incombustible membrane fabric; eventually he developed Teflon-coated fiberglass. The fabric proved to be low in cost, durable, incombustible, translucent, and self-cleaning; without the efficacy of this product it is doubtful that membrane structures of any type could have progressed to the degree that they have. With fiberglass membranes, snow loads and ponded rainwater became greater concerns than wind or rupture. In subsequent pneumatically supported membrane domes, snow is melted by pumping hot air to the membrane; backup inflation systems increase pressure when the cables slacken; and emergency roof drains automatically dump accumulated water. Geiger built twelve large air-supported stadia and sports facilities between 1974 to 1986 before turning his attention to tensegrity domes.[5]

Pneumatically supported membrane domes have been criticized because most have deflated or partially deflated owing to severe weather or mechanical failure. David Campbell, a longtime associate of Geiger's and now head of Geiger

2.3. Viewers were amazed by the size of David Geiger's low-profile pneumatic dome for Expo '70 in Osaka. (Photo courtesy Geiger Engineers.)

2.4. Walter Bird was an early proponent of inflatable structures. Here he is standing atop one of his membrane radomes. (Photo courtesy Geiger Engineers.)

### Japanese Membranes

When the Taiyo Kogyo Corporation built membrane structures for Osaka Expo '70, it relied on almost fifty years of experience in making tents. In 1966 the corporation led a university and industry study-group on the use of membranes for permanent buildings. That year the distinguished architect Masachika Murata gave credibility to the use of membranes for permanent structures when he designed, and Taiyo Kogyo engineered and built, the Miyazaki Giant Flower Pavilion, a reception facility composed of ten connected tents made of PVC-coated nylon in primary colors. Taiyo Kogyo fabricated and installed all seven of the major Expo '70 structures: the Telecommunications Pavilion was a collection of artichoke-shaped structures on stilts; the Mushroom Balloons were 30-meter-wide inflated sunscreens supported on a central pillar and stabilized by cables; the Fuji Group Pavilion, engineered by Mamoru Kawaguchi, was a structure shaped like a covered wagon, 2,000 square meters in area, composed of a dozen air-inflated hoops; the U.S. Pavilion was a cable-restrained air-inflated structure 9,500 square meters in area; the Automobile Pavilion consisted of two asymmetrical open cones supported by an exterior cable net; and the two Gates were mast-supported tensioned membranes reinforced by cable nets, 2,000 and 3,000 square meters in area, respectively. These structures represent a catalogue of all the basic types of membrane structures, and Expo '70 remains unsurpassed as the most complete collection of membrane structures. Taiyo Kogyo and its American partner Birdair remain the dominant fabricators and installers of architectural membranes in the world.

**Frei Otto**

Frei Otto was born in 1925 into a family of sculptors. His early interest in glider aircraft led to his being a fighter pilot during World War II. While a prisoner of war near Chartres, he became the camp architect, then formally continued his architecture education after the war. During a tour in the United States in 1950, Otto worked briefly at the New York office of Fred Severud, who provided the first job for many of today's creative engineers. At the time, Severud was working with Matthew Nowicki on the now-famous State Fair Arena in Raleigh, North Carolina, with the first large cable-net roof ever built.

In 1957, Otto originated the Development Centre for Lightweight Construction in Berlin, which evolved in 1964 into the Institute for Light Structures in the Faculty of Engineering at the Technical University of Stuttgart. Here Otto built, or at least studied, pneumatic and tensioned membranes, deployable membranes, retractable roofs, plate structures, and grid domes. Although Otto severed his official connection to the institute several years ago, it thrives under the direction of Ekkehard Ramm; now the institute engineers study the structural secrets of natural forms: the "self-organizing" processes of soap bubbles, crystals, radelaria and other microscopic plant and animal life, branching systems, vortexes, and such. IL, as the institute has come to be known, may be Otto's greatest legacy; hampered by the lack of a permanent membrane material, Otto focussed on theoretical issues and the training of a generation of European engineers.

In 1972, in recognition of his marvelous work for the Munich Olympics, the Museum of Modern Art in New York presented a large exhibition of Otto's work. The exhibition—which included a large tent in the museum garden hung from an A-frame—and the publications that it fostered stimulated the development of tensioned membrane structures and so propelled Frei Otto's name into the forefront of architecture that his works dominated discussion of tensile structures for years.

Engineers, notes that in the ten largest stadia "there have been a total of fifteen full deflation incidents, averaging to approximately one deflation per ten 'operating years.' However, in the last one hundred operating years, there have been only four deflations, compared to eleven in the preceding fifty-eight operating years."[6] Improvements in design and operating procedures have largely eliminated the danger of deflation (which does not necessarily damage the membrane or cause injury), and consequently Campbell feels that the continued criticism of inflation domes is unfair. Air-inflated domes have lower initial costs than steel truss domes (about half the cost) and tensegrity domes (perhaps three-quarters of the cost), although life-cycle costs are probably higher for most inflated domes than for those alternatives.[7] Nevertheless, there may well be sites, in low snow areas, for example, where an air-inflated structure would be an appropriate choice (plate 3).

In spite of improvements in the design of air-supported structures, the fear of inflation problems and the limited shapes possible have led to the adoption of membranes stretched over poles or hung from exterior supports, as in traditional tents; such structures now mainly supplant the more problematic air-supported ones. Early work in these tensioned membrane structures was heavily influenced by the cable domes of Frei Otto (box).

When Otto built the sprawling German Pavilion for the Montreal Expo of 1967, membrane material was not strong enough withstand the tensions necessary to maintain a large structure supported by only six poles. Otto relied on a network of connected steel cables to establish the surface of the tent, and he hung a fabric membrane liner just below the structural cable net. Startling and daring in its shape and in its appearance of lightness, the German Pavilion led to a similar commission with architect Gunther Behnish for the Olympic Stadium in Munich in 1972 (plates 4–5).

2.5. Teflon-coated fiberglass was first used for an architectural membrane in 1973 in constructing the Student Center at the University of La Verne, California. The building is still in use, and the membrane is lasting better than original projections foretold. Bob Campbell, engineer; John Shaver, architect. (Photo courtesy Geiger Engineers.)

After Otto won the initial design competition with a cable-net roof plan, skepticism on the part of contractors, even the steel cable contractors, about the safety of such a large cable-net nearly sank the project. Two alternatives were drawn up, with laminated wooden beams substituting for the cable net. The German Olympic commission was deciding between the plans when the cable-net design was revived with support from an unexpected source: television broadcasters. Television cameras were not then capable of adjusting to the shadows cast by thick beams; the broadcasts of the recent world championship soccer games from Mexico had been a disaster. A uniformly clear roof was thus needed. Finally, a cable net with gray-brown acrylic panels 4 millimeters thick was approved. The planners determined that the panels would satisfy the broadcasters, help protect visitors from the sun, resist ultraviolet radiation, shrink in case of fire, releasing heat and smoke, and have a reasonable life expectancy.[8]

Otto's tension-structure philosophy was joined with Geiger's Teflon-coated fiberglass membrane in 1973 by an architect and an engineer, John Shaver and Bob Campbell, for the Student Center of the University of La Verne in California (fig. 2.5). This was the first use of the fiberglass fabric developed by Geiger. The Student Center is a pole-supported permanent tent structure in which the tension is carried by the fabric, not a supporting cable-net.

The membrane is regularly examined by Birdair (Walter Bird gave this name to his company) to see how it is weathering. Birdair's conclusion is that the membrane has surpassed the projections of the fiberglass manufacturer Owens-Corning by 50 percent, retaining 70 percent of its fill yarn tensile strength and 80 percent of its original warp strength. Because loss of strength has tapered off during the past five years, the membrane is now expected to remain effective for more than thirty years.

Cross-section microphotographs comparing membrane samples of unused 1973 material with material from the La Verne structure show that the Du Pont Teflon coating is still translucent and not discolored. Teflon is chemically inert, remaining unchanged in temperatures varying from –100 degrees Fahrenheit to +450 degrees. Water, not ultraviolet radiation, has turned out to be the enemy of fiberglass. The material is long-lived when moisture is kept from the fabric. The La Verne building is thus doubly important: its successful erection demonstrated that Teflon-coated fiberglass was strong enough to be used in tensioned structures, and as the oldest constructed example using the material, it continues to prove the fabric's durability.[9]

With Skidmore, Owings, and Merrill's use of Teflon-coated fiberglass membranes for the Hajj Terminal at the King Abdullaziz International Airport in Jeddah, Saudi Arabia, in 1981, pure membranes began to be used for large-span structures (plate 6). Horst Berger, by then in partnership with David Geiger, collaborated with Fazler Khan of Skidmore, Owings, and Merrill on the conceptual design and also provided Owens-Corning, the designer and fabricator of the membrane, with a detailed engineering plan for the erection and stressing of the roofs. Berger has aptly called this huge project "a forest in the desert." With 210 units, each 45 meters long on each side, it has not only the largest membrane covering but the largest roof structure in the world, covering 430,000 square meters.

The Hajj Terminal was built to serve Muslim pilgrims who come to the holy city of Mecca in fulfillment of their religious duty to their faith; the rate of increase of visitors in the late 1970s was considered in the design. Most of the 700,000 hajjis who pass through the terminal every year arrive and leave within a thirty-day period, and the facility was planned to accommodate as many as 100,000 at one time, providing comfort and shelter for many hours until the pilgrims could continue their journey. The hajj season changes from year to year with the Muslim lunar calendar and will upon occasion take place during a time of year when temperatures in Saudi Arabia reach 130 degrees Fahrenheit (plate 7).[10]

The design solution is a series of 210 tents organized into a hierarchy of 21-tent modules and 5-module sets. Each 2,025-square-meter tent is supported by four 45-meter-high steel pylons;

each tent begins 20 meters above the floor and rises, cone shaped, to a height of 33.5 meters, where the tent peaks in metal collar opening 4.8 meters in diameter (plate 8). The openings allow a continual flow of fresh air in from the sides of the tent. The membrane covering reflects 75 percent of the solar radiation, allowing the temperature under the tents to remain in the 80s even when the exterior temperature is an extreme 130 degrees. The membrane has been fabricated so that about 7 percent of the available sunlight is transmitted, providing soft daytime illumination. (The remaining 18 percent of sunlight is absorbed by the fabric.)

To make this forest of tents rise in Jeddah, pylon towers were erected, either singly or in connected pairs or in four-pylon frames. A metal collar was suspended from every square group of four towers, and the collars were stabilized by four cables running to the mark on the pylons, 20 meters above the ground, where the lower parts of the tent units were to be attached. The tents arrived at the site completely manufactured; they were unpacked but not unfolded. Each metal collar separates into top and bottom circular parts, one of which was lowered to connect to the circular hole in a tent (fig 2.6a). When the lower collar was drawn up to the upper collar, the membrane roof unfurled fully, the lower edges of the membrane having been clamped to edge cables running from pylon to pylon (fig. 2.6b). Workers then laced thirty-two radial support cables through pockets in the deployed membrane for additional support. The final step in the assembly was to bolt the two separated parts of the collars together, stressing the membrane. Units were not stressed singly, for the pylons are too delicate to withstand the inward pull of the tensioned membrane. Instead, the 21-unit modules were all raised at once, allowing the membranes to support the pylons as the pylons simultaneously support the membranes (fig. 2.6c).[11]

Structures that support membranes are

a

b

2.6. (a) To deploy the Hajj Terminal roof, each membrane was partially unfurled and attached to a collar suspended from pylons. (b) Next, each membrane was attached to rings that would slide up the pylons. (c) Finally, by pulling each collar up to its mating collar, the membranes were fully unfurled; groups of tents were raised and stressed together. (Photos courtesy Geiger Engineers.)

c

increasingly sophisticated. A recent Berger membrane structure, perhaps the most graceful membrane structure built so far, is the Cynthia Woods Mitchell Center for the Performing Arts (also called the Woodlands Pavilion). The summer home of the Houston Symphony, it was completed in 1990 for a total budget of $9 million (plate 9). The membrane is supported by an external structure as in the Hajj Terminal, but this time Berger has chosen for support three A-frames that weave through the complexly curved membrane. The steel supporting structure is both inside and outside the building, which softens

the distinction between the interior side and the exterior side of the membrane; visitors feel that this Möbius band of a building could fold them inside while, at the same time, it projects cloistered music to the outside world.

The three A-frames of white trussed steel are arranged in a fan shape, opening out from the stage to encompass seating for 3,000. An additional 7,000 can sit on the grassy berm outside the building. The steel A-frames sit on open trussed columns so that views are not obstructed; the delicate columns cannot, however, absorb the lateral tensile forces in the membranes, so horizontal trussed struts are employed just under the membrane for this purpose (plate 10). The struts do a double duty as hangers for lights and loudspeakers. Rain is collected by the roof and shed through gutters in the columns.[12]

Control of light and sound are intrinsic to the membrane. During the day, natural light is softened as it passes through the fabric; at night the highly reflective surface is used for indirect lighting, although enough artificial light goes through the membrane to dramatize its wonderful sculptural shape. Soft fabric muffles sound, and membranes can be specially engineered as acoustical liners to reduce noise, yet tensioned membrane surfaces are excellent for reflecting sound and are even being used to focus sound where that is their only function, as in Todd Dalland's membrane for the Winter Garden in New York.[13] Tensioned membrane surfaces are anticlastic—the woof and warp lines in the weave are curved in opposite directions—and therefore diffuse sound, which allows musicians to hear one another and prevents "hot spots" of uneven sound from occurring in the audience. In the Mitchell Center the surface, because of its general shape, projects sound to the audience, reducing the need for amplification even for those outside on the berm. In fact, the original plans and budget called for an additional acoustical liner in the pavilion to project sound, the concern being the 54-foot height at the peak of the roof; but the acoustical liner has not been needed and has not been used (although report has it that chamber music is hard to hear). Light and sound take the same path around the interior and then project out to the audience. The form, the structure, the function, and the mechanical workings of the building are one.

The San Diego Convention Center, erected in 1989, was envisioned by the architect Arthur Erikson as a giant archaic ship docked at San Diego Bay (plate 11). Masts, sails, cables, and spars were part of his original imagery, and Horst Berger and Birdair were hired to see that his conception came to pass. Unlike at the Hajj Terminal, the membrane is supported by interior poles. These tent poles do not reach the ground, however; they are supported 28 feet off the floor by cables hung from exterior concrete buttresses, which resemble the flying buttresses of Gothic cathedrals or perhaps the ribs of an old wooden ship. The result is an open span 300 feet square covered by a flying tent roof. Struts painted blue and cables covered in red plastic limn the white sails against a blue sky, even from inside: when on a yacht, people smile (plate 12). Berger considers this structure the most beautiful of his projects.

Winds from the bay create uplift, and Berger used the concrete buttresses to anchor the valley cables that hold the membrane down and trim (fig. 2.7). The membrane peaks are supported by poles that cannot also be hung directly from the buttresses but must be centered between them. In an astounding architectural gesture, pairs of poles are supported by cables to become flying struts, and these cables separate and themselves fly between two buttresses. With open ends, large openings along the sides, and openings in the top to allow for the release of hot air, the structure has little visible means of support. A fly cover is suspended from the tops of the masts, preventing rain from entering the openings in the main membrane; its use further dematerializes the roof, which is one of overlapping, discontinuous surfaces (plate 13). The open ends are made possible by a "tuning fork" truss hung between the row of posts down the length of the membrane. As in the Mitchell Center this truss structure stretches the membrane along its length, and eliminates the need for external support of lateral forces in that direction, and, also

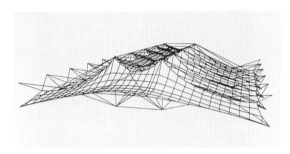

2.7. The canopy of the San Diego Convention Center is held up by flying struts and held down by valley cables. Horst Berger, engineer; Arthur Erikson Architects, architect. (Drawing courtesy Horst Berger.)

as in the Mitchell Center, the truss can support lights and speakers.[14]

Although the membrane partially ripped in one windstorm and membrane panels had to be replaced, the roof has been a success. It is easy to maintain: the convention center purchased a box of detergent, but not once has the roof been cleaned; the occasional rain washes off any accumulated dirt. Once, earthquake shocks were strong enough to shake down ceiling tiles in the building, but the membrane roof required no adjusting. The building is cool in the summer and warmer during the winter months. Under the tent, the sound of large gatherings is muffled. The structure, a favorite of San Diego residents, is in demand for bookings. Indeed, it has become the Sydney Opera House of San Diego: the one building that identifies the city in the minds of outsiders. Its reflection on the water at night, dominating the shoreline with its graceful lines, promotes the comparison.[15]

Technically, the Jeddah and San Diego membranes are canopies, not part of enclosed buildings, and they have been erected in warm climates. Neither tests the full potential of membranes to provide shelter. In the Lindsay Park Aquatic Centre, completed in 1983, Geiger and his associate David Campbell prove that membranes can both be translucent and contain fill insulation, and thus provide shelter in extremely cold climates. The three-and-a-half-acre facility,

which includes swimming and diving pools, is in Calgary, Alberta (plate 14). Remarkably, the roof provides a thermal insulation (R) value calculated to be between 16 and 20 and still transmits 4 percent of the available sunlight. Four percent is enough to illuminate the facility without artificial light during the day, as well as provide light for substantial plantings. A value of R16 is comparable to that provided by many rigid buildings whose roofs weigh twenty times as much; uninsulated membrane has an R value of about 1, and double membranes whose insulation is only a layer of air have R values of about 7. At Lindsay Park, there are as many as four layers of membrane filled with translucent fiber wool (Sheerfill II, Teflon/Fiberglass from Chemfab) supported by a 420-foot metal truss arch. David Campbell thinks the limits of performance for insulated membranes have not been reached: with more translucent silicone-coated membranes and more layers, R values could surpass 24 and possibly even 30. The Lindsay membrane also represents an improvement in sound insulation; a very thin plastic vapor barrier beneath the insulation conducts sound into the insulation, where it is absorbed.[16]

The Denver International Airport project confirms the practical advantages of tensioned membranes for long-span enclosures in cold climates (plate 15). Original plans called for a hard roof, and the approved design was passed to C. W. Fentress, J. H. Bradburn and Associates, the firm given the responsibility for producing the building. The architects doubted that the building could be completed on schedule, and estimated that the roof would put the building $48 million over budget (an outside consultant estimated $72 million over budget), so they proposed, and began to design, a membrane roof. The problem fell into Berger's lap. A design concept for a roof 1,000 feet long and 220 feet wide was produced in twenty days, and production drawings were ready in seven months. Because the roof could go up before the side and end walls, Berger estimates that being able to work inside earlier in the construction schedule recouped four or five months.[17]

The architect James Bradburn wanted the airport, like the great train stations of Europe, to infuse the traveler with a sense of place, not be an anonymous structure that could have been plunked down anywhere. To him, because Denver represents open sky and mountains and history of tipi architecture, a membrane roof was the obvious aesthetic as well as practical choice (plate 16). Even on a cloudy day the membrane passes approximately 200 foot-candles of light, three times the illumination in an average office building; moreover, the light is complete. (Bradburn learned the value of full-spectrum illumination when he was architect for renovations to the Metropolitan Museum of Art in New York.)

Teflon-coated fiberglass membrane transmits the full spectrum of visible light, cutting only the infrared and ultraviolet ends of the spectrum. The result is an interior space that gives occupants the unmistakable feeling of lightness, of being outside while inside. The illusion is furthered by the modulation of light due to the inner liner, which varies from 16 inches to 9 feet in its separation from the outer liner, giving a softness to the "sky." In a strange way, noon and dusk both seem like full illumination, no doubt because the light is diffused by the membrane: without sharp highlights or glare, the eye can adjust to low light levels.[18]

The feeling of being outside did not come without effort. Talc is used on the fiberglass filaments to permit a tighter weave. Although it is washed off, some remains, and it caramelizes when the fabric is heated during the coating processes. The fresh membrane is shipped with a murky beige color. Ultraviolet radiation bleaches a membrane spanking white in a few weeks to a few months, but an interior membrane liner is shaded from ultraviolet rays by the exterior membrane. A good deal of extra work was need-

ed to bleach the liner membrane chemically before it was installed.

But Denver is in the mountains! In fact, snow fell heavily after the roof was installed and before it was prestressed (when a fabric roof is at its weakest) without ill effects. The fabric roof, complete with clamps and with cables 3 inches in diameter, weighs less than 2 pounds per square foot, yet it can support snow loads twenty or even thirty times as heavy (fig. 2.8). If the roof were a steel spaceframe, it would weigh an estimated 30 pounds per square foot, and a steel and concrete structure that size would weigh 80 to 100 pounds per square foot. Prestressing is a three-month-long process of pulling down on the lowest points of the roof. The snow that does not slide off the slick prestressed roof neither

2.8. Lowering the "octopus" nodes stresses the roof of the Denver International Airport. Horst Berger, Severud Associates, roof engineer; C. W. Fentress, J. H. Bradburn and Associates, architects. (Photo: Tony Robbin.)

2.9. At the Denver airport, the curving glass wall is freestanding, secured to the movable roof by flexible air-inflated sausages. The choice of architectural membrane kept construction under budget and ahead of schedule; only the automatic baggage-handling system delayed the opening of the airport. (Photo: Tony Robbin.)

deforms the membrane nor is visible to people looking up through the inner liner.

The roof is capable of large deflections— several feet under wind loads, for example—and the problem of connecting the moving roof with the stationary glass end and side walls was solved in an imaginative way. Packed between

glass and membrane are inflated air "sausages" capable of distorting their shape while maintaining heat insulation and lessening the transference of shock to the glass (fig. 2.9). The inflation of the sausages is maintained by air pumps even though holes permit them to collapse as needed. The sausages are somewhat inelegant in appearance, but they are covered by an inner liner membrane maintained about 24 inches from the roof membrane. The liner membrane not only hides awkward fittings but provides thermal and acoustical insulation as well.

The membrane and inner liner together allow 7 percent of the sunlight on the roof to enter; the walls of the airport are glass, and the combination of membrane and glass provides more than enough daylight illumination without artificial lighting. The highly reflective membrane reduces heat buildup due to sunlight, yet its translucency also permits heat discharge at night, reducing the load on air conditioning. As Bradburn explains it, the volume of a building increases by a cube function as surface area increases by a square function. Heat (from lights, machinery, and people) builds up, and the accumulated heat has relatively little surface area through which to radiate. (It is expected, for example, that the Denver airport will have to be actively heated only two weeks a year.) Membrane structures reduce the heat load by their 75 percent reflective surface, by the low mass of the roof itself—there is little to hold absorbed heat—and by reduction of the need for artificial illumination, which produces more heat than light. Thus, according to Berger, "only the heating load on winter nights is higher than for a conventional building." With the membrane, then, instead of a conventional roof, for both heating and the greater problem of cooling the "net result is a substantial savings in energy consumption and operating costs while producing a more comfortable and attractive interior environment."[19]

As with all large membranes, the roof

arrived from the factory in precut panels. These were laced together by cables running though hinge-shaped clamps. After the membrane was lifted into place, the seams were covered with a flap that was heat-welded to both edges of the membrane, turning the roof into one seamless panel. Birdair has discovered that there is no substitute for building a physical model of the roof to rehearse the steps needed to safely erect masts and riggings, and to position cranes so that they can snake through temporary supporting rigging to lift the fabric. There were seventeen such operations, one for each bay of the building; each bay/membrane took approximately one week to install, unless winds greater than 20 miles per hour halted work. In all, the "fabrication and construction of the roof system took the efforts of more than 300 people, over a time period of approximately three years."[20] The roof is estimated to have cost about $65 a square foot; a precise figure is not available because Birdair bid the roof and the side and end walls in one contract. Given that the $4 billion project was completed so quickly, compared to much longer periods for smaller airports in the United States and Japan (at costs of up to $18 billion), the Denver roof will certainly be emulated for many years.

One more membrane building is worth presenting in some detail: a three-story structure in Venafro, 73 kilometers northwest of Naples, that Philippe Samyn built to house a chemical industry research facility. Samyn is ideally suited to work with membranes, having trained first as an engineer and then as an architect. The most important requirement for the facility was that the building be flexible in its use; its owner did not want to be burdened with a building that could not accommodate a future large-scale experiment, especially an expensive building not easily reconfigured and certainly not one for which he would have to wait to use. Samyn's solution was to design an arch-supported membrane structure 85 by 32 by 15 meters in size and

containing no interior columns. The building was designed so that it could be built in six months, and in fact construction began in July 1990 and the building was occupied in early March 1991, eight months later. Inside the membrane there are administrative and research "boxcars," self-contained, air-conditioned, trailer-type units that can be rearranged in the large open space without too much difficulty (fig. 2.10). Samyn has thus redefined the "flexible" building to mean not a large, heavy building with movable partitions but a large membrane-enclosed space with small movable rooms inside.[21]

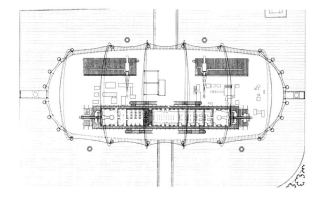

a

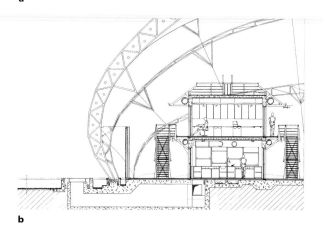

b

2.10. The (a) plan and (b) section of Philippe Samyn's M & G Research Laboratory in Venafro show self-contained "boxcar" rooms inside a clear-span membrane structure. (Drawing courtesy Philippe Samyn.)

1. Madrid's Palacio de Cristal was built by the architect Velázquez Bosco in 1887. The engineering innovations of standard cast parts, rigid portal frame connections, and tension tie rods permitted a new aesthetics of the open span. (Photo: Ben Van Tongeren, Cruquius.)

2. Hard materials are no guarantee of permanence. (Photo: Tony Robbin.)

3. The Tokyo Dome, an air-inflated structure, was built in 1988. When it was used for a rock concert, images were projected on the clear span roof. Takenaka Corporation/Nikken Sekkei, engineer and designer; Taiyo Kogyo Corporation, roof fabricator and installer. (Photo: Yokio Yoshimura, courtesy Geiger Engineers.)

4. In the Olympic Stadium built in Munich in 1972, cable nets support acrylic panels. Frei Otto, engineer; Gunther Behnish, architect. (Photo: Ben Van Tongeren, Cruquius.)

5. A detail of the Munich cable net shows the compound curvature that keeps all parts of the net in tension. (Photo courtesy Geiger Engineers.)

6. The Hajj Terminal at the King Abdulaziz International Airport is designed to accommodate 100,000 Muslim pilgrims at a time. Skidmore, Owings, and Merrill, architect and engineer; Horst Berger, consulting engineer; Birdair, membrane installer. (Photo: Jay Langlois, Image Source, Toledo, Ohio.)

7. The interior of the Hajj Terminal, shaded and ventilated by the canopy, remains in the 80s although the temperature outside can be as high at 130 degrees Fahrenheit. (Photo: Jay Langlois, Image Source, Toledo, Ohio.)

8. The Hajj Terminal testifies to the beauty as well as the practicality of membranes. (Photo: Jay Langlois, Image Source, Toledo, Ohio.)

9. The Cynthia Woods Mitchell Center for the Performing Arts in the Woodlands, Texas, completed in 1990, has a beautiful, sound-projecting shape. Horst Berger, architect and engineer; Birdair, membrane fabricator and installer. (Photo: Robert Reck, courtesy Birdair.)

10. In the Mitchell Center, trusses stretch the membrane horizontally, eliminating the need for cables and anchors outside the covered space. (Photo: Robert Reck, courtesy Birdair.)

11. The San Diego Convention Center, completed in 1989, uses the delightful imagery of the harbor: lines, sails, and spars. Horst Berger Partners, roof engineer; Arthur Erikson Architects, architect; Birdair, membrane fabricator and installer. (Photo: Robert Reck, courtesy Birdair.)

12. Under the convention center canopy, people feel as though they are on a yacht. (Photo: Tony Robbin.)

13. The tuning fork truss removes the need for cables and anchors at the ends; the fly cover allows for openings in the main roof. (Photo courtesy San Diego Convention Center.)

14. The Lindsay Park Aquatic Centre in Calgary, completed in 1983, is light enough inside for plants to grow and warm enough for people to swim. David Geiger and associates, engineers; Chandler Kennedy Architectural Group, architect; Birdair, roof fabricator and installer. (Photo: L. Webster, courtesy Geiger Engineers.)

15. In the Denver International Airport, completed in 1994, the mast heights are varied, enlivening the profile of the roof. Horst Berger, Severud Associates, roof engineer; C. W. Fentress, J. H. Bradburn and Associates, architect; Birdair, membrane fabricator and installer. (Photo: Robert Reck, courtesy Birdair.)

16. The full-spectrum light and open-sky feeling identify the interior of the airport with Denver. (Photo: Robert Reck, courtesy Birdair.)

17. The M & G Research Laboratory in Venafro, Italy, uses a reflecting pool for cooling and security. Samyn and Partners, architect and engineer. (Photo: Matteo Piazza, courtesy Samyn and Partners.)

18. The Pompano Beach (Florida) Bandshell, completed in 1993, is a charming play of geometry. John Williams, engineer; Jeff Falkanger and Associates, architect; Birdair, fabricator and installer. (Photo: Robert Reck, courtesy Birdair.)

19. Detail of the Pompano Beach Bandshell. (Photo: Robert Reck, courtesy Birdair.)

20. The membrane for Detroit's graceful Chene Park Amphitheater was installed in 1990. Schervish, Vogel, Mertz, designer and architect; Kent Hubbell Architects, fabric architect; Birdair, membrane fabricator and installer. (Photo: Robert Reck, courtesy Birdair.)

21. The Folkstone Chunnel Terminal, completed in 1993, shows that tensioned membrane surfaces need not be symmetrical. Building Design Group, architect; Birdair, fabricator and installer. (Photo: QA Photos, courtesy Birdair.)

2.11. The interior of the M & G laboratory is both light and cool. (Photo: Matteo Piazza, courtesy Philippe Samyn.)

The choice of a membrane structure suits site as well as building use. In southern Italy the summer sun is hot, and the white membrane with 2 percent transparency provides cool shade (fig. 2.11). Air intake and outtake systems at the far ends of the oval structure further cool the building, and the overall shape of the membrane assists in the movement of air. Strikingly, Samyn has placed the building in the center of a reflecting pond (plate 17). Air brought into the building has been cooled by evaporating pondwater, providing natural air conditioning. The pond provides additional security for the research center. Finally, the site is known for earthquakes. A membrane structure is capable of absorbing tremors with less damage than a rigid structure,

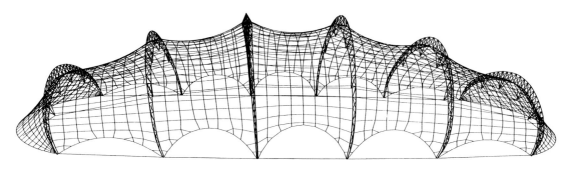

2.12. The trussed arches of the Venafro facility are not parallel but radiate from a common line; the trusses are turned to make graceful slopes with the membrane. (Drawing courtesy Philippe Samyn.)

and it is extremely lightweight. Samyn gives the weight of the roof at 15 kilograms per square meter for a roof calculated to be able to support 150 kilograms per square meter.

Six steel trestle arches hold up the PVC-coated polyester membrane (fig. 2.12). The arches are not perpendicular to the ground but aligned as radii of very large circle and held in place by six longitudinal cables in tension. The cables and the arches are a self-supporting unit not dependent on the membrane for stability. (Two escape hatches are precut in the membrane for the emergency evacuation of the building, which is one way the integrity of the membrane could be violated.) Samyn admits to overriding engineering decisions for architectural reasons. The trussed arches, for example, are triangular in section, and a more logical engineering choice would have been to place the flat side uppermost and hang the membrane from inside the arch, attached to the inward ridge. Such a design lacks finesse; instead, Samyn rotated the triangular sections of arch so that the roof swoops to delicate points, the membrane attaching to the flat underside. He has also understood and exploited one of the most visually rich properties of membranes; they are screens for shadows, and shadows can be projected on or through them. He has oriented his building east-west, making the arches into a giant sundial; workers can observe the

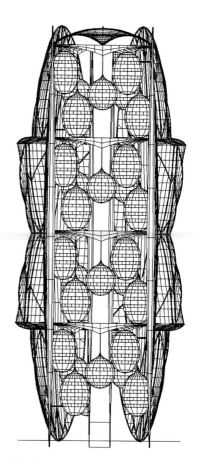

2.13. José María Baquero and Bruce Danzinger's Grape Vine proposal to make high-rise apartment buildings out of membranes won the Taiyo Kogyo Corporation's competition for new ideas for using membranes. (Drawing courtesy Bruce Danzinger.)

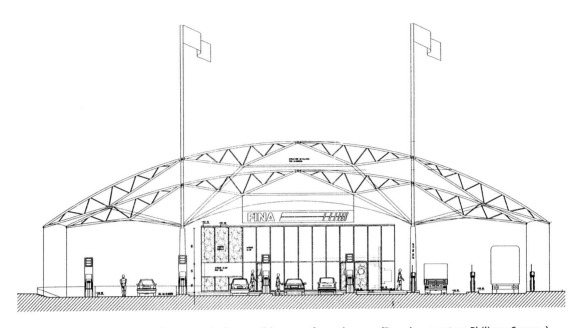

2.14. Philippe Samyn's gas station expands the possible uses of membranes. (Drawing courtesy Philippe Samyn.)

passage of the sun from the changing patterns on the membrane.

The Venafro research facility is important in the history of membrane structures because of its use by a private company; it is not a stadium or other public building. Samyn's structure shows that soon perhaps membranes will have expanded applications—even housing, as in the Grape Vine proposal put forward by the engineer Bruce Danzinger and the architect José María Baquero (fig. 2.13)—and that the economic and practical advantages of membrane can be maintained at a modest scale.[22] Indeed, Samyn has recently completed a Fina Petrol station with an arched-truss-supported membrane (fig. 2.14). The Venafro facility also proves that membranes can be used in applications in which security is a prime consideration. Like the beautiful Mitchell Center, the Venafro structure is successful because the membrane constitutes the whole building; it is not just a roof tacked onto a conventional building. As with the San Diego facility, the membrane was conceived by an architect at

the beginning of the design process, and the hard parts of the structure were built around the soft parts.

Membranes do not divide space into inside and outside so much as they fuse inside and outside; they provide a biological-type filter that passes attributes of the outside to the inside, and vice versa. As in Berger's Möbius-band building, membranes can make the transition from outside to inside seamless. They can control climate and sound without the need for walls, doors, air locks. When people talk about the aesthetics of membrane structures, they usually mean fussing with the details of cable nodes and fasteners or, at best, keeping the graceful shape of tensioned membranes visible. As we have seen, membranes are aesthetically successful when they are the building, not just the roof. But the true aesthetic potential of membranes has just begun to be exploited (plates 18–21; fig. 2.15). Just as steel and glass forced the aesthetics of open-plan architecture, membranes force a redefinition of inside and outside space: enclosure without cloister. Now we have been given a taste for open, curved, interior spaces that are bathed in light and seem roofless, thereby connecting us to the sky. Such delightful new tastes can become a craving, and when that happens, membranes will no longer be considered materials for special structures but will instead be considered as natural as wood, steel, and glass.

2.15. The central pillar supporting the Folkestone Chunnel Terminal roof (see plate 21) is a flying strut that does not reach the ground. (Photo: QA Photos, courtesy Birdair.)

# Tensegrity

When the French engineer René Motro built a lightweight membrane structure in the south of France, trucks brought tons of concrete to the site. How could the structure be called lightweight? his client wanted to know. The innocent question became a koan that led Motro to study tensegrity structures. Tension structures must be attached somewhere; otherwise, the tension disappears and the membrane flies away. These structures are usually attached to the ground; earth is the weight that keeps the membrane tight. But making the connection between earth and membrane is not easy, and massive concrete anchors below ground are often needed (fig. 3.1).[1] Tensegrity systems are self-anchored, however; they pull only against themselves. Such structures are self-stressed in a "closed" system.

Tension and compression are almost always found together in a structure. A beam supported at the ends is stretched along its bottom edge and compressed along its top edge. The keystone of a dome is pressed into place, but at the base of the dome, accumulated lateral thrust pulls the building blocks apart unless they are contained by a tension ring (such as an iron chain). Strictly speaking, no material fails in compression; a column of marble is crushed when its surface fails in tension, no longer able to contain the pressure built up in its interior. The challenge of efficient structures is to use geometry such that tension components are made of pure tension materials,

such as cables, while only compression components are made of bulkier compression materials. Tensegrity systems are the purest expression of this principle: in a pure tensegrity structure the compression members do not touch, and relatively few compression members (struts) are suspended in a net of pure tension members. Buckminster Fuller defines tensegrity as "small islands [of compression] in a sea of tension."[2]

The first examples of what came to be called tensegrity structures were made by a Russian artist, Karl Ioganson, and presented in the Obmokhu Exhibition of 1921. Ioganson was a founding member of the First Working Group of Constructivists and a party to the first exciting discussions on replacing composition (artistic, intuitive, and oriented to taste) with construction (progressive, oriented to technology and engineering). "From painting to sculpture, from sculpture to construction, from construction to technology and invention—this is my chosen path, and will surely be the ultimate goal of every revolutionary artist," he wrote in 1921. In his 1920 *Study in Balance*, now lost and known only through photos and descriptions, Ioganson balanced three leaning, nontouching compression posts with a continuous tension string running through the hollow posts and from vertex to vertex (fig. 3.2). As Lásló Moholy-Nagy later explained, pulling the string would change the position of the posts, although the structure

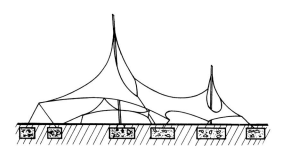

3.1. Lightweight tensioned-membrane structures need heavy anchors. (Drawing courtesy René Motro.)

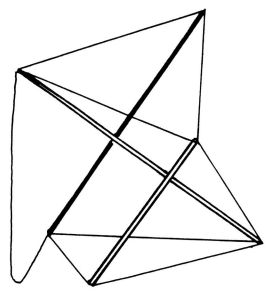

3.2. In Karl Ioganson's sculpture *Study in Balance*, exhibited in 1921, compression members do not touch and are held in position by tension cords. (Drawing courtesy René Motro.)

would remain in equilibrium. Christina Lodder, a scholar of the period, has speculated that given Ioganson's desire to integrate his art with the material goals of the Revolution, his sculptures had a "utilitarian imperative" and were meant to be models of "utilitarian structures such as portable, fold-up kiosks or collapsible items of furniture."[3]

Unfortunately, the promise of this idea was not recognized in Russia, and tensegrity structures can be said to have been invented by the sculptor Kenneth Snelson in 1948 in response to a semester of study with Buckminster Fuller. Fuller, an inventor, immediately saw the potential of Snelson's idea, named it, improved upon it, campaigned for its acceptance, and ultimately patented his version of it, in 1962. Although the idea fascinated architects and engineers from the time a tensegrity structure was first exhibited at the Museum of Modern Art in 1959, and although Snelson went on to make a great reputation for himself building large-scale tensegrity sculptures, the assumption persisted until recently that tensegrity was not practical for large-scale permanent structures (plate 22; box on tensegrity units).[4]

Fuller shows in his patent how to use tensegrity to build a single-layer dome, the first application of pure tensegrity to architecture

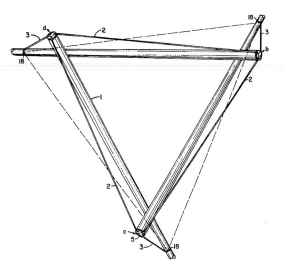

3.3. Buckminster Fuller's basic tensegrity unit is a collapsed octahedron with three cables attached to the ends of each rod instead of four. (Drawing: U.S. Patent Office.)

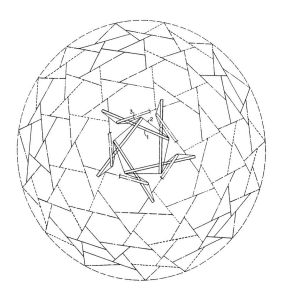

3.4. Fuller first applied tensegrity to a single-layer dome. (Drawing: U.S. Patent Office.)

(figs. 3.3–3.4; box on dome). Three struts are connected by six cables such that the ends of the struts do not intersect, making a "tensegrity."

The configuration, whose origin is "a tripod as in an Indian tepee," "displays the six vertexes which are characteristic of the octahedron."[5] Leaving out cables makes the three-dimensional tensegrity lie almost flat, and joining the ends of some of the booms together in a color-coded pattern makes a surface of hexagons, pentagons, and triangles that can be wrapped around a sphere. Fuller describes a 270-boom configuration based on a six-frequency subdivision of an icosahedron, a configuration often used in his geodesic domes (each side is divided into six parts): As the twenty triangular faces of the icosahedron are subdivided into smaller triangles they can be expanded outward to more and more closely approximate the surface of a sphere. (The pentagons are located on the "sphere" where the twelve vertices of the original icosahedron were; five triangular sides of the octahedron come together at a point. The flat triangular sides are broken up into regular triangular nets, which automatically make hexagonal patterns.)[6]

David George Emmerich, of the Ecole National Supérieure des Beaux-Arts, seems to be

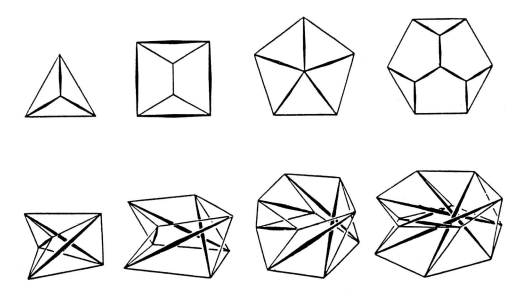

3.5. Antiprism tensegrity units can be made with struts as diagonals between prism ends that are cables. (Drawing courtesy David George Emmerich.)

## Snelson's Tensegrity Units

Snelson's dramatic sculptures have a great variety of shapes and feelings: some are ordered, symmetrical, and frontal; others corkscrew through space in unpredictable ways. Elegant needle towers, as high as 90 feet (see plate 22), are part of his oeuvre, as are sprawling, horizontal sculptures with massive components. Surprisingly, the variety results from mastery of only a few basic geometric insights, described in Snelson's patent 3,169,611, submitted in March 1960 and granted in February 1965.

In the patent, Snelson's first tensegrity unit is a simple diamond kite: two bars crossed at the middle, with tension cords around the four endpoints. Such a kite is quite strong in its plane (when lying on the floor) but is unstable in the third dimension (when stood on edge). Two such kite-planes become stable when intersected. Owing to the crossing of the bars, each kite has a left-handed and a right-handed aspect, and matching the left-handed side of a kite to a right-handed side of another kite facilitates the separation of the crossed kite bars; the two-dimensional kites can be drawn open to make four-bar units with true three-dimensional tensegrity. Once the four-bar units are established, they can be elongated and assembled in a great variety of ways. The outer hull of the assemblies can be semiregular Archimedean solids, like a cuboctahedron (the intersection of a cube and an octahedron, made up of six squares and eight triangles) or a truncated octahedron (with six squares and eight hexagons). Alternatively, by varying cable and rod lengths, seemingly random or organic forms can be made.

The second major unit for Snelson is the triangular prism: two triangle ends are matched up, and three flat sides join the two ends. This is the common prism that Newton used in his experiments on the rainbow

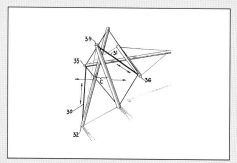

Example of Snelson's "kite" unit. Similar units inspired the first use of tensegrity in architectural applications by Buckminster Fuller. (Drawing: U.S. Patent Office.)

*Easy Landing* (1977), a stainless steel sculpture by Snelson. (Collection of the City of Baltimore; photo courtesy Kenneth Snelson.)

diffraction of light. Such a prism can be made from from six cables and three rods, the triangular ends being made of cables and the long parallel lines made of bars. Constructed this way, the prism is unstable, and it remains so when placed end up so that the rods splay apart. However, adding three stressed cables from the bottom of each rod to the top of an adjacent rod solidifies the entire structure; the rigid bars now become the diagonals of the rectilinear faces of the regular prism now made up of cables. An additional three cables from the bottoms of the rods to the midpoints of the upper cable triangle increases rigidity.

The prism sections can be stacked vertically by placing the rod ends of the next upper course at the point where the two cable are joined. Although still a straight prism, each configuration looks rotated and, indeed, tends to rotate either clockwise or counterclockwise as it collapses. If the units are stacked left-handed version over right-handed version, the rotation is damped out of the structure. The result is a tower of triangular prisms in which rods maintain a maximum distance from each other, both at their ends and at their midpoints. By varying cable and rod lengths, the towers can sweep to a sharp point, remain a constant column, or undulate as stacked hourglass shapes.

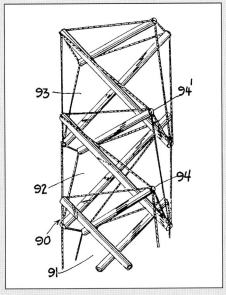

Triangular antiprism tensegrity units, stacked by Snelson to make a tower. (Drawing: U.S. Patent Office.)

the first to have pointed out the possibilities of generating double-layer tensegrity grids by using antiprisms. A triangular antiprism is a prism whose two triangular ends are rotated with respect to one another; now the sides are not flat rectangles but folded, making two triangular faces where before there was only a rectangle. Both triangular ends can be cables; clockwise spokes can be bars; and counterclockwise spokes can be cables. Three cables in tension fix the ends of each bar. The antiprisms need not be triangular, and four-sided or five-sided ends can be used (or ends with any other number of sides); indeed, the two ends of the antiprism do not have to be the same size but could, instead, terminate a tapered figure. Beginning with a French patent of 1964, Emmerich has pioneered the use of these tensegrity antiprisms to make double or multilayered grids.[7] His work is important in its efficient use of bars. By using compression bars as the diagonals of tensegrity units rather than as edges, as Fuller proposed, all space-filling grids can be made with only one-fourth of the members as compression members, saving weight and materials costs (fig. 3.5).

Emmerich is also important for his study of minimal bar lengths. He has found ways to combine prismatic tensegrity units into toroidal rings so that the torii packings provide a rotational stability to the prisms that they would not have on their own (fig. 3.6).[8] As a result of this synergetic combination of units, the prisms can be regular prisms as opposed to antiprisms, and as a consequence of this squaring of the prism's faces, the prism's diagonals—which must be compression members—can approach their minimum length in relation to the edges of the face, which are tension members.[9] Ratios of bar length to cable length are important in making tensegrity structures efficient.

If *tensegrity* is to mean anything, says Snelson, it must refer to systems where the compression members do not touch, as in his own work or as in Fuller's single-layer dome. His

## The Dome at Katowice

Under the heading "Architectural Archeology" or perhaps "Patents Are Silly" place the following item. The Polish-born engineer Waclaw Zalewski—the uncredited inventor of several structural innovations later made famous by others who had the good fortune to build in the West—designed and built the first tensegrity dome for a 12,000-seat sports arena between 1960 and 1962 in Katowice. Zalewski began the dome before Fuller filed his patent for an aspension dome and completed it before Fuller's patent was granted (see below); this was twenty-six years before David Geiger's first tensegrity domes, which were thought to have been the first ever built. The Katowice roof, a span of 400 feet, is larger than Geiger's first efforts, and it is slanted, like the Thunderdome in Saint Petersburg, Florida. The stadium is built in the coalmining region of Silesia, where multiple underground tunnels make large-footprint buildings treacherous. Zelewski therefore made the overall shape an inverted bowl, with the outward thrust of the slanted walls creating the compression-ring effect needed to balance the inward tension of the tensegrity roof. Zalewski chose a twelve-hoop system, with posts 3 meters high supporting the metal roof and the central high-arched dome. The profile of the building has given the stadium its nickname: Flying Saucer Arena.

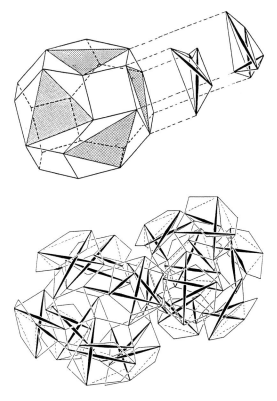

3.6. Antiprisms stacked in a closed form have a tendency to rotate but are prevented from doing so by other antiprisms in counterrotation. (Drawing courtesy David George Emmerich.)

admonishment notwithstanding, I find that if we are willing to consider impure and hybrid tensegrity designs, greater efficiency is possible with only a modest loss of magic.

Ariel Hanaor, of the Israeli Building Research Institute, notes that in tensegrity configurations the bars in a unit can be brought close together. If they are connected at this point, by welding them together or by using a rigid joint, the length of the bar is effectively halved, and bars with thinner cross-sections can be used. (Reducing the length of a bar by half increases its resistance to bending by a factor of four.) Thus, relatively thin units shaped something like jacks could float in a net of thin cables and arch

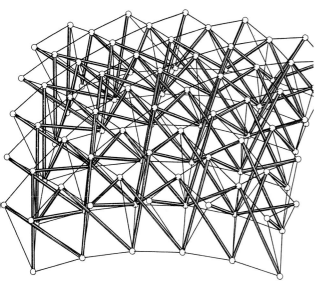

3.7. In René Motro's modified double-layer truss, two square cable grids are held apart by diagonal struts that meet at nodes. (Drawing courtesy René Motro.)

overhead to support a roof. Hanaor studied a dome of this type and found that it has less weight than even a conventional double-layer grid truss (box).

In another example of an impure but effective tensegrity system, Motro, who is director of the Civil Engineering Laboratory at the University of Montpellier–II, joins bars together at their ends to make a double-layer tensegrity domed grid (plate 23). As with Emmerich's double-layer tensegrity grids, the top and bottom surfaces are composed entirely of cables; compressive bars are only in the diagonal struts between these cable-net surfaces. The innovation in Motro's work is to join some bars together at their ends (fig. 3.7). The connected bars form continuous zigzags; these rows of diagonal trusses (without rigid top or bottom cords) intersect on the bottom layer. Here is the configuration: four bars meet at a node on the bottom, only two nodes met at the top, the bottom cables form an

## Hanaor on Tensegrity Grids

Ariel Hanaor studied double-layer tensegrity grids as substitutes for double-layer flat trusses and domes. He compared a geometrically flexible plane grid (made up of triangular antiprism tensegrity units), a rigid plane grid (octahedral tensegrity units), a flexible dome configuration (triangular antiprisms), and a rigid dome configuration (octahedral tensegrity units).

He found that standard double-layer truss systems are more rigid than any tensegrity system, but rigid dome tensegrity configurations are almost as stiff as the conventional octet truss; in fact, they are stiff enough to support rigid cladding—a consideration important for architecture. Flexible tensegrity plane grids (flat trusses) are the least efficient, even though they have the fewest cables and are visually the most open. This is because they require greater prestressing in the cables, because greater prestressing requires heavier bars, and because the heavy bars (struts) must be the longest members (the diagonals) of the units. Rigid plane configurations have more cables but can support with lighter struts. Even in the most efficient tensegrity configurations, he says, compression elements (those vulnerable to buckling) must be the longest members—more than twice the length of the tension members in antiprism configurations—and thus a fundamental inefficiency is built into the system.

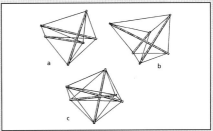

Three ways to make a three-strut tensegrity unit. Only tensegrity c, the completed octahedron, is technically rigid. (Drawing courtesy Ariel Hanaor.)

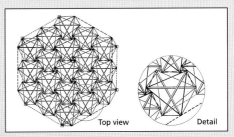

Rigid plane tensegrity grid employed in Hanaor's analytic and physical model tests. (Drawing courtesy Ariel Hanaor.)

Buckminster Fuller's comparison of his aspension dome with a Japanese lantern is a wonderful example of engineering by metaphor, something for which Frank Lloyd Wright was also famous. Lore has it that Wright conceived the hollow, funnel-shaped columns of the S. C. Johnson and Sons building as lily flowers supporting hummingbirds at rest and that he thought the sprawling Imperial Hotel should be balanced on its platform like dishes on a waiter's tray. Fuller imagined roofs in a variety of lantern shapes: his patent enumerates square hoop domes, as well as rhombs, hexagons, and even irregular shapes. One idea in Fuller's patent that has not been tried is the use of "sheets, plates, or panels" in place of hoops and posts, an idea also suggested by lanterns. In a later writing the tensegrity patent is also introduced by a metaphor: A tensegrity dome is like an atom or solar system in that the elements do not touch but are held together by "tensional coherence" forces, such as gravity. "Nothing in the universe touches. The Greeks misassumed that there was something called a solid. . . . Today we know that the electron is as remote from its nucleus as is the Earth from the Moon in respect to their diameters. We know that macrocosmically none of the celestial bodies touches each other. So, both microcosmically and macrocosmically nothing touches."

almost square net, as do the top cables, except that the top square net is rotated with respect to the bottom net. The top and bottom cable nets are made with continuous single lengths of cables, rather than with separate pieces running from node to node; separate pieces, a complication of many tensegrity systems, adds to the expense of fabrication. Curvature is generated by varying the interval between bars on the continuous cable running between nodes; all the bars are the same length.[10]

The great advantage of Motro's tensegrity dome is that it cleans up the busy nest of cables, connectors, and rod ends that obscure the geometry of the tensegrity domes of Fuller and even those of Vilnay, Emmerich, and Hanaor. As we have seen, in these purer configurations three bars often approach each other, visually overlapping from every vantage point, and each end has at least some very short cables running to an adjacent bar end. In Motro's example, rows of bars are connected only at delicate pivot points, and the bars are spaced equally far apart. That they do not rotate or splay apart is captivating. The visual simplicity of the system more than compensates for the joining of some bars at their ends.[11]

In 1964, Fuller patented his "aspension dome" system, so named for an ascending suspension structure in which inner hoops are hung from posts erected on outer hoops (fig. 3.8). That is to say, a hoop is hung from cables attached to the top walls of the structure. On the hoop, posts are erected, and from these posts hang more cables, which support a smaller inner hoop, again with posts attached. Yet a third hoop is erected in this manner, so that a relatively flat dome is defined, consisting primarily of tension cables. Although Fuller is silent on the subject of the covering, it is obvious that the roof could be a lightweight, translucent, watertight membrane, miraculously held rigid by just a few struts, none of which reach to the ground. By way of introducing this patent in a later book, Fuller wrote:

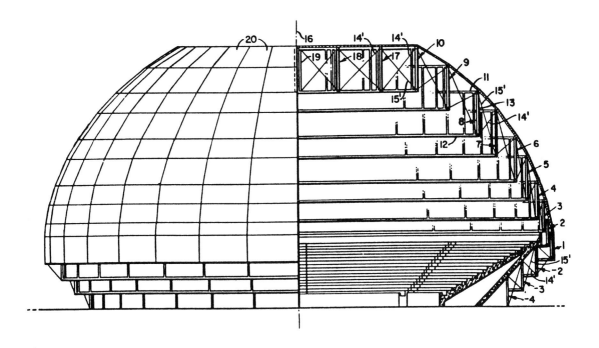

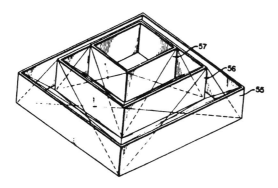

3.8. In Fuller's aspension dome, each ascending course of posts (or compression plates) is suspended from the top of a lower, larger one. (Drawing: U.S. Patent Office.)

"I found in the world of tensegrity it was also feasible to produce what I call the aspension dome, a dome that could be progressively assembled on the ground from its maximum-diameter base and continually hoisted aloft. This is really an alternative to the tensegrity geodesics. It has an accordion-opening effect such as the foldable Japanese lantern, which can be progressively pulled open to provide space" (box).[12]

Fuller's aspension dome system fails to meet the definition of tensegrity in two major ways: it is not a "closed" system, but depends on a strong compression ring around the perimeter (at the top of the seats, say, if the dome is a stadium), and, second, vertical posts (compression members) are attached to rather substantial hoops, which, even though made of a collection of rods or cables, have the appearance of post-on-beam construction, an unfortunate illusion amplified by the common practice of placing catwalks on the hoops. On the other hand, these "hoop domes" or "Cabledomes," as Geiger has called them, were developed by Fuller at just the moment when tensegrity was being worked out by Snelson and Fuller, and, as Fuller states in his patent application, the ideas were interdependent in his mind. People who view the domes are, in any case, strongly reminded of tensegrity structures like Snelson's sculptures. See, for example, Masao Saitoh's Amagi Dome, where delicate spiderwebs of cables are kept apart by a few short struts in a gossamer mist (plate 24). I think we can fairly call aspension domes tensegrity domes, and consider them the first architectural application of tensegrity. It may even be possible to make hoop domes without hoops, which would make them even more like other tensegrity grids; Horst Berger has long proposed suspending two-strut pairs on cables that span an outer compression ring. Berger proposed such a structure for the Suncoast Dome (discussed below).[13]

Fuller missed seeing the realization of his idea by only five years. David Geiger completed four of these tensegrity domes in the few short years between the start of construction for the 1988 Seoul Olympics and his untimely death in October 1989. For Geiger, tensegrity was a way to support fabric roofs without the expense of mechanically inflating pneumatic supporting structures and without the concomitant dangers of deflation due to mechanical failure or excessive snow loads (fig. 3.9). Working with the architects Kim Swoo-Guen and Kang Kum-Hee, Geiger cut his teeth on two small domes in Seoul: a three-hoop gymnastics arena 393 feet in diameter and a two-hoop fencing stadium 295 feet in diameter. The membranes are silicone-coated fiberglass fabricated by DCI. Inside the membranes are an 8-inch-thick insulation bag, a vapor barrier, and an acoustical liner (which is simply zipped into place with a standard zipper). Geiger must have been reassured that the domes could support unbalanced loads, like drifting snow, when he realized that approximately 25 tons of equipment—lighting, catwalks, cameras—were hung from single points of the structure. In general, aspension domes are remarkably strong for their weight. The full snow load, as prescribed by the building code in Normal, Illinois, for example, is 25 pounds per square foot. Geiger's Redbird Arena, 65,000 square feet large (in the plan), is in Normal and meets the code specifications (plate 25). It can bear a total load greater than 800 tons, which is more than ten times the self-weight of 65 tons, or 2 pounds per square foot.[14]

Geiger domes are not triangulated, as Fuller

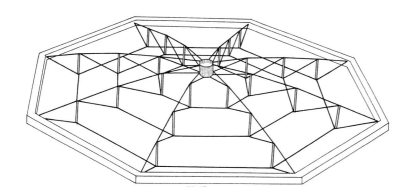

3.9. David Geiger's cable domes do not have triangulating cables; they have only radiating cable trusses and hoop cables. (Drawing courtesy Geiger Engineers.)

3.10. (a) A construction photo of David Geiger's Gymnastic Hall for the Korean Olympics in 1988 shows that the structure is stable without the membrane covering. (b) Detail of the hoops and struts. (Photos courtesy Geiger Engineers.)

proposed. Here, triangulation means that the ends of each post are rigidly held in place by being at the vertex of a triangle of supports. Rather, the struts and cables form vertical plane trusses, set on ascending hoops (fig. 3.10a; plate 26). The structures are stable without the membrane roof; and the membrane is added after all the cables and struts are set. Geiger said: "We realized that the triangulation was not a necessary part of the cable structure. It adds a redundancy and a fine tuning that you do not need and creates problems" (fig. 3.10b). Indeed, under some loading conditions, as Campbell has shown, triangulation concentrates the load on a few cables, whereas without triangulation the

membrane can do its work and spread the load over a wide area. But nontriangulated domes can be quite rigid under uniform loads, deflecting as little as 235 millimeters, or $1/474$ of a 120-meter span, under wind suction, as Campbell has also shown.[15]

With the Suncoast Dome, now called the Thunderdome, the architects Hellmuth, Obata, and Kassabaum proved that large-scale tensegrity domes are not only feasible but cost-effective. Saint Petersburg, Florida, is the site of this tensegrity dome, 690 feet in diameter, which was engineered by Geiger and completed in 1989. The compression ring of the dome slants from 225 feet to 85 feet, reducing the volume of air to

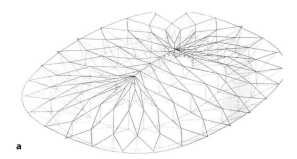

a

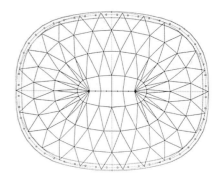

b

3.11. (a) For the Georgia Dome, Matthys Levy returns to Fuller's triangulated tensegrity dome system and adds hypar shapes to the membrane panels. (b) Oval plan of the Georgia Dome. (Drawings courtesy Matthys Levy, Weidlinger Associates.)

be cooled while maintaining a shape compatible with its primary use as a baseball stadium. Four hoops are used for the structure, and these are supported by an interesting innovation. The ridge cables are really clusters of cables, and at the top of each post some cables separate from the cluster and become the diagonal cables supporting the next innermost ring. The advantage of this system is that each hoop is hung, indirectly, from the compression ring, and the ridge cables become progressively lighter toward the center of the dome. The roof is designed to prevent ponding, and a collateral benefit of the valley and ridge configuration of the wedge-shaped membrane panels between posts is a continuous downward run to the exterior of the building, even though the roof is quite flat: rain flows right off the roof.[16]

The 1987 bid of $37.93 per square foot of clear span (excluding catwalks) is higher than for a comparable air-supported dome on this site (about $31.00 per square foot, according to Geiger's estimate). When insurance costs (if available), operator costs, and increased heating and cooling costs are all included, tensegrity domes are nevertheless competitive with air-supported structures. Furthermore, a greater percentage of the cost of tensegrity domes is labor than is the case with air-supported structures,

meaning that in countries with lower labor costs, tensegrity domes become more economical.[17]

In Atlanta's Georgia Dome, Matthys Levy and his coworkers at Weidlinger Associates return to Fuller's original triangulated formulation (plate 27). At 784 feet the Georgia Dome is the longest tensegrity span yet made. In this design, ridge cables do not run straight from the compression ring to the top of the dome, making wedge-shaped panels, but instead crisscross the roof, making rhombs. The triangulated design also means that from the top of each post two cables, not one, descend to support the next innermost hoop, forming a tension triangle. Levy was concerned that the large, noncircular hoops might tend to rotate without triangulation. The result of his design, however, is a stiff roof. The deflection of only 2 feet over the short span of 700 feet is considered stiff enough for a plaster ceiling![18]

With triangulation, as many as six cables join at a single node; they must approach the exact geometric center of the top of the post. Because the cables lie in two planes, on either side of the post, it seemed natural to design the nodes as a weldment of two plates. The nodes are massive, weighing as much as 2 tons, and the most economical way to make them is with two welded plates or single bent plates (plate 28).

The dome is the home of the Atlanta Falcons football team, and a football stadium requires an elongated shape. Being curved at every point, an ellipse might have provided more stability to the structure while encompassing the long rectangle of the football field. But in the triangulated system of an elliptical plan, every node has cables coming to it from slightly different directions. To simplify and standardize the node design—of critical importance for cost-effective design—Levy chose an oval plan of two circles joined by a "butterfly section" (fig. 3.11). Because the two circles tend to separate, they must be joined by a vertical planar truss. In keeping with the tension-cable spirit of the structure, and because both the top cord and the bottom cord are in tension, the planar truss is a cable truss: two cables kept apart by steel posts that are in compression.

Levy's innovation is to use hyperbolic paraboloid shapes for the membrane roof. Hypars, as they have come to be called, are saddle shapes: the curvature up in one direction intersects the curvature down in the perpendicular dimension. The complex curvature of hypars ensures that every part of the surface is in tension without the need of valley cables pulling down on the membrane panels. The hypar sections are established by a simple device: "lifting two opposite corners and dropping the other two corners of the diamond. The overall surface of the roof maintains a downward slope to ensure rainwater drainage toward the edges."[19]

Hanging the first hoop far below the compression ring at the top of the stadium would interfere with the view of spectators sitting in the top rows. On the other hand, a shallow angle, which would raise the hoop, increases the tension in the cables and the compression ring from which that first hoop is hung. It was discovered that a 45-degree angle is optimal and that each subsequent inner ring could have a shallower angle because each carries less load. Other variables in the design are the number and width of each panel (which affects the number of posts and the amount of tension in each panel of fabric), the height of each post (which affects the depth of the roof and the degree of tension in the cables), and the number of rings, or stages (which affects the number of connectors). The cost of the roof without fabric was assumed to break down thus: 50 percent for cables, 20 percent for posts, and 30 percent for connectors. Juggling these factors with what is known about the performance of the Teflon-coated fabric, Levy selected a three-ring system with fabric panels less than 100 feet wide and a post height that would give the roof its relatively flat profile. Optimization studies that take into account the labor costs of handling the connections, which increase with the number of rings, and the fabricating costs of a large number of short cables suggest that fewer ring-hoop systems are more efficient.[20]

Now at least eight tensegrity domes have been built, and the engineering of such structures is maturing. Their efficiency and beauty ensure that more will be erected. A great variety of shapes and applications will ultimately become part of our architectural tradition, as the artists Ioganson and Snelson first imagined.

# Deployable Structures

An old problem for designers is how to avoid building structures twice: once in the form of a wasteful, dangerous, temporary scaffolding and again in the final material. In 1419, Filippo Brunelleschi designed a way to build the Duomo in Florence without wooden centering; designers from the time of Ramses II, in the thirteenth century B.C.E., have built pitched-brick barrel vaults for the same reason. Now new technology fully solves the problem of how to build a roof when there is not already one to stand on: the technology of deployable structures. A distinction must be made here between prefabrication and deployment, for all architecture is prefabricated to some degree; ore for steel girders is not mined, smelted, or forged at a Manhattan building site. Deployment concerns not the premanufacture of elements but the more or less complete pre-assembly of an entire structure in a factory, the collapsing of the structure for shipping, and the unfurling, or deploying, of the structure on site.

Buckminster Fuller was an early and influential proponent of deployable architecture. He was impressed with the American automobile industry, which used centralized and standardized production methods to build complex machines—for 25 cents per pound in 1928. Fuller thought that such techniques could be applied to housing in place of "craft" production methods and that housing, too, could be built for 25 cents a pound. This was Fuller's real motivation for his often-misunderstood question to architects: "What does your building weigh?" The problem, of course, was how to deliver such "Dymaxion" houses from the factory. Fuller first imagined airship delivery; later, in the 1950s, he proposed a "seedpod" system in which geodesic domes folding by a scissor mechanism would be delivered by rocket and would erect themselves on impact.[1]

According to Colonel Henry C. Lane of the U.S. Marine Corps, writing in 1958, Fuller's deployable-structures "principle is particularly suited to military shelter development and is the first major basic improvement in mobile military shelters in the past 2600 years." Lane said that geodesic domes, even without a scissor or seed-pod mechanism, required only 3 percent of the weight of other military shelters, 6 percent of the volume, 14 percent of the cost, and 1 percent of the labor-hours for erection. Compared with tents, for example, Fuller's domes were 75 percent lighter in weight and and took 88 percent less time to erect, yet could withstand 150-mile-an-hour winds, which tents could not do. Fuller spun out other possibilities: one-third domes dropped as parachutes, structures weighing one-thousandth of what traditional housing weighs, and scissor-mechanism membrane-covered domes deploying with compressed air in fifteen minutes. Lane concluded that geodesic domes "could be used for 89% to 99% of Marine Aviation shelter needs" (box).[2]

The architect and sculptor Bernard

## Outer Space Structures

In the 1980s, when the United States thought that it would build a space station, the National Aeronautics and Space Administration funded research in deployable structures. The idea was to fabricate foldable engineering systems that could fit into the space shuttle's cargo bay for transport to orbit and then to deploy, or "explode," these structures to ten or more times their length. Such grand dreams have been downsized since then, but there still is a need for small structures in outer space and for such other deployable objects as antennas and solar collectors.

Sergio Pellegrino, of Cambridge University, has made a deployable ring of rods joined at their midpoints by pivots, passive cables strung between the ends of some rods, and active cables running through some rods and strung between the ends of others that are recoiled in deployment. The rods make a scissor mechanism. When the active cable is drawn in—wound around a drum with an electric motor, for example—the structure opens until the passive cables are taut. It could be used for an antenna disk.

Koryo Miura and his colleagues at the Institute of Space and Aeronautical Science in Japan combine sophisticated mathematics and the traditional craft of origami to make planar deployable systems. A compactly folded surface can be flattened out if it has zero local curvature, that is, if the folds make parallelograms and if the sum of the angles around every point is 360 degrees. This mathematical definition of flatness (zero local curvature) refers only to the planar angles on the surface, so there is no tensile stress across the surface due to folding, other than stresses at the folds. The optimum parallelograms in Miura's planar deployable systems have acute angles of approximately 84

degrees, which allow for important improvements over right-angle folding: (1) an interdependent accordion fold in two directions, which means that pulling in one diagonal direction unfolds the sheet in two dimensions; (2) once deployed, the sheet does not have a tendency to recoil on its own owing to spring stresses in the sheet, again because of the two interdependent folds; and (3) the sheet is not required to bend around multiple thicknesses, greatly reducing stresses in the sheet. Miura's invention allows for a repeatable deployment of a two-dimensional sheet (such as a solar collector in space) by extending a single telescoping rod.

Other wildly imaginative research has been done; some ideas, involving the creative use of exotic materials, are described in a box in Chapter 8.

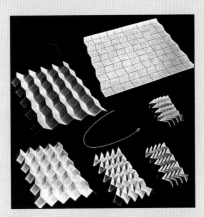

Deployable planar systems, the product of both mathematics and origami. (Photo courtesy Koryo Miura.)

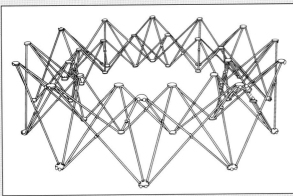

Scissor mechanism used for a deployable ring.
(Drawing courtesy Sergio Pellegrino.)

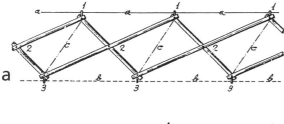

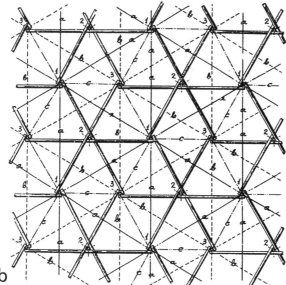

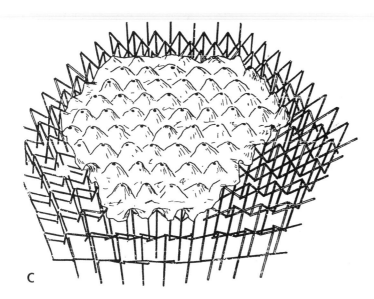

4.1. In the early 1960s, Emilio Piñero pioneered the use of scissor mechanisms to make deployable structures. A mechanism can expand (a) in a horizontal direction, (b) in both horizontal and vertical directions, and (c) with a fabric covering, which unfolds with the mechanism to complete a deployable roof. (Drawings: U.S. Patent Office.)

4.2. Piñero displays his prototype of a deployable shell. (Photos courtesy Félix Escrig Pallarés.)

Kirschenbaum, who made the first geodesic dome house and developed the geodesic radome, has said that weather predictions at the geodesic dome sites in northern Canada were good for only twenty-six hours, so that the domes had to be assembled by a few people in twenty hours to be safe from harsh storms destroying the incomplete assembly. One technique that gains speed is to assemble the center arch flat on the ground, stand it up, and repeat the process with smaller outer arches.[3]

In 1961 the Spanish architect Emilio Pérez Piñero, encouraged by Fuller, developed a full-size foldable theater, each large section of which arrived at the site on a single wheelbarrow and was then unfolded with a scissor mechanism. In a scissor mechanism, often called a pantograph, each rod has three pivot joints, one on each end and one toward the middle. As two ends of a pantograph are brought together, the center pivots are spread apart, lengthening the mechanism as a whole. In Piñero's drawing of a planar pantograph, what is gained in length in the horizontal direction is the sum of what is lost in depth in the vertical direction in each unit of the mechanism. As Piñero explains in his U.S. patent, when a pantograph that is three-dimensional in its stowed state deploys to a planar square pattern, the new area covered is approximately the square of the length gained—a startling difference in folded and extended size (fig. 4.1).[4]

Piñero realized that the scissor mechanism could make hexagonal patterns if three rods, not two, were joined at each pivot point. He envisioned covering his pantographs with a tensile membrane not only to create shelter but to secure the mechanism. He also realized that if the interior pivot point on a rod was not at the midpoint, then the pantograph generated a curved surface, "a shell-shaped configuration." For the Salvador Dalí museum in Figueras, Piñero proposed an unfolding roof of square panes of glass that Dalí was to paint. The roof was not completed owing to Piñero's death, but

the idea of a pantograph mechanism with rigid square panels is being studied again by his followers. Piñero is almost forgotten outside Spain; sometimes architects and engineers in other countries fail to cite his work or are genuinely ignorant of it. Yet Piñero, working in the early 1960s, was apparently the first to develop many implementations of scissor mechanisms and to build large-scale, working deployable structures (fig. 4.2).[5]

Félix Escrig Pallarés of the Escuela de Arquitectura de Sevilla and Juan Pérez Valcárcel of the Escuela de Arquitectura de La Coruña have continued the study of pantograph structures in Spain. They have replicated and improved upon Piñero's work and considered the geometric shapes possible with the scissors device, including compactly folded geodesic spheres and the icosahedra on which they are based (fig. 4.3). Their most important work,

4.3. The scissor mechanism developed by Félix Escrig Pallarés for deployable architecture is based on Piñero's. (Photos courtesy Félix Escrig Pallarés.)

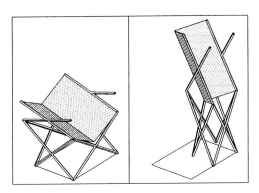

4.4. Pantograph mechanism roofs incorporating rigid panels—a design developed by Escrig Pallarés and Juan Pérez Valcárcel—can be used for long, light-weight spans. (Drawing courtesy Félix Escrig Pallarés.)

however, is the analysis, computer modeling, and prototyping of pantographs that incorporate rigid-plate roofing elements. Generally, fully folded deployable structures have either a thin fabric roof attached or none at all. Membranes used in deployable structures may foul, degrade with multiple use, and fail to contribute to structural strength. Escrig Pallarés and his coworkers have determined that they are useful only in reduced spans.[6] With rigid plates as part of the mechanism—plates that overlap one another like the scales of a fish and that are fixed in place once the mechanism is opened—it is possible to greatly reduce the total weight per unit area (fig. 4.4). As a span increases from 20 meters to 60 meters, the weight per square meter of structure falls, given the added strength of the plates and the resulting thinness of the mechanism elements. In fact, for a 60-meter steel span without plates the weight per square meter is calculated to be about 24 kilograms, whereas the same structure incorporating rigid plates would weigh about 5 kilograms per square meter, plus the weight of the plates.

Triangle, square, and rhomb panel shapes are possible. Triangle shapes interfere with one another at the last stages of folding, but Escrig Pallarés suggests partial deployment on the ground, attachment of the panels, and then fur-

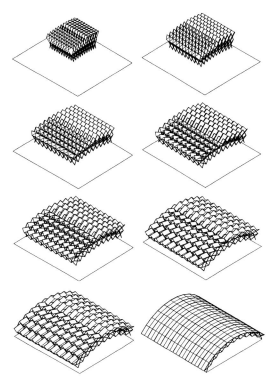

4.5. A deployable vault by Escrig Pallarés and J. P. Valcárcel compacts to a small area. (Drawing courtesy Félix Escrig Pallarés.)

ther deployment from a crane. Systems with squares and folded rectangles can form flat trusses or more structurally efficient cylindrical domes. What is remarkable about all these deployable structures is how tightly they compact. As we can see in figure 4.5, which shows the process in reverse, a cylindrical truss flattens out as it collapses. This somewhat mysterious flattening movement is also seen in pantograph domes with triangular faces, and the flattening is a boon for packing. Folded rhombs can be in a variety of shapes, and unfolding mechanisms in which each panel is slightly different are also possible.

Inspired by Piñero and Escrig Pallarés, Y. Rosenfeld and his coworkers at the Technion in Israel have made a prototype of an arch 2 meters

## Chuck Hoberman

Chuck Hoberman, sculptor and engineer, has created an impressive example of the pantograph mechanism that operates in three dimensions. By bending scissor members at the central pivot and by moving that pivot point off the line of the end pivots, he has designed pantographs that form smooth curves. His geodesic sphere hanging in the atrium of the Liberty Science Center in New Jersey easily expands from 4½ feet to 18 feet in diameter. Two scissor elements, each with four bars, separate every two nodes of the dome, effectively doubling the pantograph of Piñero. Each node of the fully deployed structure has a top plate and a bottom plate that come together when the pantograph members are extended, and when the two plates are locked together, the structure is rigid. In stowed position the two plates of the node are at their maximum distance from one another; the bottom plates are brought together at the center of the sphere while the top plates project out like porcupine quills. The mechanism can be engineered so that the dome expands when only one cable is pulled (U.S. patents 4,942,700 and 5,024,031).

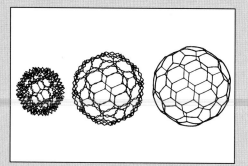

Hoberman's deployable geodesic sphere.
(Drawing: U.S. Patent Office.)

in radius. When collapsed, the arch bundles to 1.8 by 0.3 by 0.15 meters and weighs approximately 20 kilograms. Two workers can deploy the arch in about twenty seconds; parts simply click into place to lock the arch rigid. More than 100 deployments have proved the reliability of this configuration of rectangular units that are cross-braced and that have structural depth (although they cannot be called true double-layer grids). These arches can be ganged together to form barrel vaults and covered with a flexible membrane. Like Escrig Pallarés, Rosenfeld has a computer program for folding structures. Rosenfeld's program calculates the dimensions of the rods and the location of the pivot points when given the parameters that define the overall shape and the number of units that make up the pattern. With continuing research on scissor-mechanism deployable structures in universities in Spain and Israel, as well as in the United States, Belgium, Mexico, Venezuela, it seems as though the seed planted by Piñero thirty years ago has taken root and sent out shoots (box).[7]

Ariel Hanaor, the Israeli engineer who has studied double-layer tensegrity grids so thoroughly, has extended his research to include deployable examples—specifically, by elongating telescoping struts in a pure tensegrity system (where struts are connected only to cables). The elongation is accomplished either mechanically, by turning a screw, or hydraulically or pneumatically, by pumping oil or air into the struts. Hanaor constructed two test models using the air-pressure method: a seven-unit geometrically flexible shallow dome and a three-unit flat slab. These modest examples exposed the potential problems of deployable tensegrity structures. To fold compactly the collapsed struts have to be less than or equal to the cables in length. Thick cables have limited ductility, which can also prevent compact packing. Although the cables do not seem to knot, they can become snagged on joints if the joints are not smooth. Geometrically rigid configurations (in the shape of complete octahedra), though generally preferred because of their increased structural efficiency, require exact cable and bar lengths, whereas geometrically flexible configurations (triangular antiprisms) can self-adjust their shape by means of their internal mechanisms. Rigid configurations are additionally problematic because they have more cables to compact. Still, they have relatively longer cables, so packing problems due to the strut-cable ratio do not arise. Hanaor was encouraged by his crude bench models, which deployed easily from compact packings, although limited prestressing made them weak.[8]

Since it is possible to build architecture in a deployable manner, do we have the right to ask construction workers to work any other way? Mamoru Kawaguchi, an engineer at Hosei University, distinguishes between "hierarchical" and "democratic" construction systems. In a hierarchical roof, minor beams transfer loads to intermediate beams, which transfer loads to major beams. This means that major beams can be constructed first and, once constructed, provide secure support for workers and materials. But node and rod spaceframes, the long-span roofing systems commonly used today, are democratic; they are not structurally stable until all components are in place. The safest way to work with such systems is to build them on the ground and then to lift them all at once by cranes, but this is impractical for large structures and infeasible for domed roofs, which do not lie flat.[9] Often, scaffolding must be built first, but to be useful, scaffolding must not only be safe but accurately match the dimensions of the building, adding to the expense and time of construction. The evolution of building systems has made buildings more dangerous to build at the same time society is more sensitive to worker safety; it is intolerable for people to die just so a building can be erected.

Fuller was aware of these problems with the spaceframe system that he so effectively promoted, and tried two clever construction methods to avoid the use of scaffolding or massive cranes. In 1957, for a dome in Honolulu, Fuller began by erecting a temporary tower from which cables were hung. The cables were attached to the top of the dome and used to gradually lift it as work on the dome proceeded, "enabling the assembly work to be done along the periphery of the dome always on the ground."[10] Another of Fuller's ideas was to gradually inflate a balloon as support for a partially completed dome, a method successfully used for the 384-foot dome at Wood River in 1959 (fig. 4.6). As the balloon inflates, it raises the part of the dome just completed, allowing

a

b

4.6. For a geodesic dome at Wood River, Illinois, Fuller raised the completed part of the assembly on an inflating balloon so that work could continue at ground level: (a) in progress; (b) completed. The dome, which is 354 feet in diameter, was constructed during the winter of 1958–59. (Photos: a, © 1960, and b, © 1995, by Allegra Fuller Snyder, courtesy Buckminster Fuller Institute, Santa Barbara.)

workers on the ground access to the underside of
the structure in progress. These methods never
caught on; no doubt they were as cumbersome
as more traditional practices. Yet the principle
that they suggest is sound, and the problem that
they address has not gone away.

Kawaguchi's solution to the democracy
problem is the Pantadome system, and it takes
away the breath of engineers whenever he presents it (fig. 4.7). The basic idea is to temporarily
remove certain hoops from a spaceframe dome,
replacing its triangulation with foldable rhombic
mechanisms. Although three hinges need to be
introduced for each fold, they are the simplest
kind, allowing only one degree of movement, and
such hinges, even very large ones, can easily be
made strong and precise. The dome can now be
assembled at or near ground level, including the
installation and inspection of electrical and

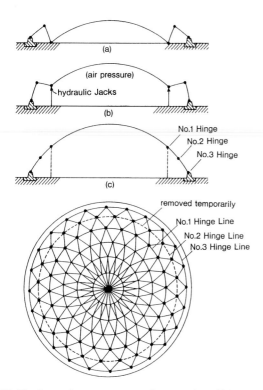

4.7. The Pantadome system employs a series of hinges
so that the completed dome can be raised all at once.
(Drawing courtesy Mamoru Kawaguchi.)

4.8. Mamoru Kawaguchi's first Pantadome was the
World Memorial Hall in Kobe, built in 1985. The pho-
tos show the erection sequence. (Photos courtesy
Mamoru Kawaguchi.)

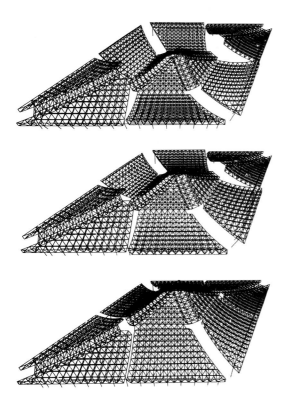

4.9. Kawaguchi and Kenzo Tange collaborated on this rhombic plan Pantadome, assembled as shown. (Drawing courtesy Mamoru Kawaguchi.)

the passing of the seasons, and snows come and go as the roof gradually rises amid a forest of cranes. Not so here: the building is raised in a matter of days (fig. 4.8). A second example, made with the architect Kenzo Tange, shows that the system does not require a circular or oval plan (fig. 4.9). This indoor stadium is rhombic, 200 by 120 meters along its diagonals. As in all of Kawaguchi's Pantadomes, the seven sections of this roof were lifted by hydraulic jacks at the same time. Indeed, the deployment system requires that all sections be lifted at once to preserve structural stability during deployment and to prevent the hinges from binding. Great care is taken that all the jacks are coordinated by a central control.

The roof of the Palau Sant Jordi, designed by Arata Isozaki and Kawaguchi for the Barcelona Olympics in 1992 and built by the Orona Corporation, measures 128 by 106 meters and consists of approximately 10,000 tubes in a double-layer spaceframe grid 2.5 meters deep and 1,000 tons heavy (plate 30). The roof is shaped by five undulating sections, which lift the roof to its maximum height of 45 meters off the arena floor. Erection of such a massive and complicated roof in the air would be difficult and expensive. Instead the roof was constructed against the bowl formed by the seating terraces and the arena floor (figs. 4.10–4.11). When assembled, the hinged roof sections were lifted all at one time by twenty-four hydraulic lifting jacks. Between November 22 and December 2, 1988, the roof was pushed up, additional 3.04-meter sections of the temporary support towers being added from below as the hydraulic jacks lifted the roof. Once the roof was raised to its full height and the missing members welded into place, the hydraulic system and temporary towers were dismantled. Although the hinges remain in place, the completion of the interrupted hoops prevents their operation. In an impressive confirmation of the stability of the system, the vertical displacement of the center of the roof was a

mechanical systems. Lifting can be accomplished with hydraulic jacks or even by air inflation of the interior space. Because the system allows only one degree of freedom of movement, the building is stable during the erection process, and lateral supports or staying wires are not needed. When erection is complete, the missing hoop members can be installed and the hydraulic jacks removed.

The first example of Kawaguchi's system was the World Memorial Hall in Kobe, designed in collaboration with the architect Mitsumune in 1985 (plate 29). The oval plan of the hall is 70 by 110 meters, rather large for a first attempt. The series of erection photographs is remarkable for what is not there; usually such sequences display

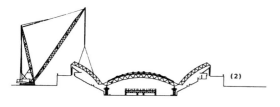

scant 140 millimeters when the lifting towers were removed.[11]

The original plans called for a roof to be completely covered with roofing material. When Isozaki saw the Pantadome system, however, he wanted to preserve traces of the deployment, so he glazed the folds, keeping them visible (plate 31). Now, in what will surely become a paradigm for future architecture, viewers can know by looking at the building that it was constructed in a rational and safe manner. The undulating shape of the roof itself, initially proposed to reflect the mountains in the background, has a more compelling, and sufficient, rationale in the Pantadome system: the arcs are formed by the rigid sections of the deployment. In the future,

4.10. Kawaguchi and Arata Isozaki's Pantadome in Barcelona, the Palau Sant Jordi, was built in the bowl formed by the risers and arena floor, then raised with jacks and temporary support towers. (Drawing courtesy Mamoru Kawaguchi.)

4.11. The roof of the Palau Sant Jordi was lifted in 1988 in just ten days. (Photos courtesy Mamoru Kawaguchi.)

we will be satisfied with such composite shapes if we know their derivation and their history in the construction process (box).

Implicit in the Pantadome system is the possibility of adjustable buildings or interactive buildings that change shape with use. It is true that there are buildings with retractable roofs—for example, the Toronto Skydome, completed in 1989, with its system of massive retractable sliding roof panels.[12] And more elegant systems have been proposed, such as the iris-shaped enclosures first designed by Piñero (fig. 4.12) and the retractable membrane for New Jersey's Giants Stadium proposed by Geiger Engineers (fig. 4.13). But Kawaguchi imagines a more fundamentally adjustable building. Roofs of large stadia could be stepped down for small events or lowered for acoustical concerts. Buildings could change shape at different times of year or perhaps even flatten between uses to minimize heating or cooling costs. At present, says Kawaguchi, there is no technological obstacle to creating such buildings, only obstacles in the form of building codes, and once the practicality of adjustable buildings has been demonstrated, the capability will surely be exploited.

Masao Saitoh thinks of his deployable structures as "performance pieces." The audience of a construction project sees a dramatic change in the structure every day. His Izumo dome—a structure 140 meters in diameter and 49 meters in height—was erected in 1992 in only eight days by the Kajima Corporation (plates 32–34). Saitoh, who teaches at Nihon University, worked with the Kajima Corporation to make a 1:20 scale model to test the procedure before beginning construction. Wood was the material of choice because the city of Izumo is famous for its ancient wooden shrines. The wooden ribs of the dome were pushed up a central pillar the way one opens a bamboo umbrella. After the ribs were pushed up, the central column was removed: the performance was over, the audience amazed. Here is how it was done: Wooden

arches were assembled on the ground and laid out as the spokes of a flat wheel. At the hub, the ribs were attached with a pivoting pin joint to a central ring. The other ends of the ribs were attached to rails, like a temporary railroad track. After the ribs were completely assembled in this configuration, and membranes attached to adjacent pairs of ribs, the sections were erected by pushing up the central ring along a temporary mast and gathering up the bottom ends of the ribs by sliding them along the rails.[13]

Safety is a large part of Saitoh's motivation in developing deployable structures. Safety for the workers and also safety for the partially assembled structure is enhanced when roofs can be built on the ground: parts can be properly braced until fastened in place, wind forces are low, and little danger is posed if a cable fails when stretched. Until tensegrity structures are fully assembled and stressed, they are especially unstable; they vibrate in wind, members rock and spin unpredictably when stood upon, and ends of cables and membranes can whip around with fatal consequences.

The massive concrete walls of Saitoh's Amagi gymnasium in Shuzenji (see plate 24), built in 1991, provide a cocoon for the assembly of the relatively small tensegrity roof (43 meters in diameter). Because of the small size of the structure, it was possible to assemble the roof on the floor of the gym after the walls were built. The metamorphosis took place when the entire and completed roof was lifted into place in one day and set upon the walls: the diaphanous yet resilient butterfly roof was pulled from its cocoon. A temporary ring was attached to the tensegrity roof for the lifting process. Once the tensegrity roof was set upon the top of the walls, sixteen V-shaped rocker arms could be winched tight against the walls. As these sixteen rocker arms rotated outward, all the cables in the roof were put in tension, seizing up the roof, and the temporary restraining collar could be safely removed.[14]

## How to Construct a Tensegrity Dome

Tensegrity domes can be built without scaffolding in a manner that might be called deployable. David Geiger's patent (4,736,553, filed on December 8, 1986, and granted on April 12, 1988) demonstrates that ease of construction without scaffolding was part of the original motivation for creating these domes. Here is how the Georgia Dome was erected, as the engineer, Matthys Levy, expounds (see plates 28–29; figs. 3.17–3.18). The uppermost cable net, the ridge net, was laid out on the ground. Cables had been marked with paint to locate the position of connectors. Next the cable truss, which connects the two circular halves, was laid on the ground, with movable concrete pads used as temporary bases. This truss was lifted vertical and plumb and attached to the ridge net. Now the ridge

net was ready for lifting; it was pulled up with temporary lifting cables running from fifty-two points on the concrete compression ring. With the ridge net lying inverted, shaped like a bowl, the next set of cables and the outermost of the three hoops was laid out on the playing field. This structure was lifted under the roof net in the same way. Posts (vertical struts) were lifted by cranes (two at a time on opposite sides of the roof), attached to the ridge net, and lifted farther until they could be set onto the hoop. The roof line was raised still higher, but it still dipped inward like the crater of a volcano. The sequence was repeated two more times: the next inner hoop was raised and its posts lifted and attached, then the last hoop was installed. Finally the fabric panels, which arrived from Birdair rolled on drums, were lifted by cranes above the places where they were to be attached. After one corner of the fabric was fixed into place, the drum was unrolled over that section of the dome, and the rest of the fabric was attached.

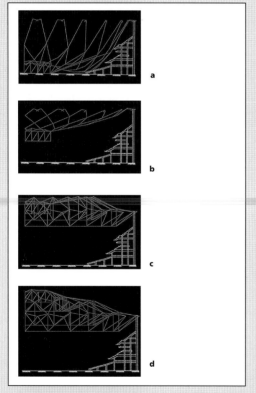

Erection of Levy's Georgia Dome: first, the ridge cables were laid out on the ground; next (a–b) the ridge-cable net was raised to its inverted position with the central cable truss attached; then (c–d) the ridge net was raised and tensioned as hoops and struts were pulled under it. (Drawings courtesy Matthys Levy, Weidlinger Associates.)

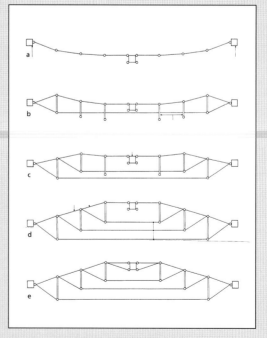

In Geiger's tensegrity domes, (a) the upper cables are hung, then (b) a hoop and struts are hung, raising the inverted ridge cables; (c–e) more hoops and struts further raise and tension the ridge cables. (Drawing courtesy Geiger Engineers.)

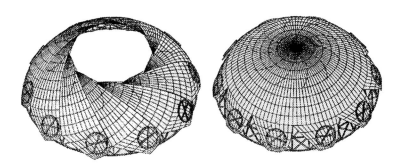

4.12. Piñero's retractable dome, circa 1961, opens and closes like the iris of an eye or the aperture of a camera. (Drawing courtesy Félix Escrig Pallarés.)

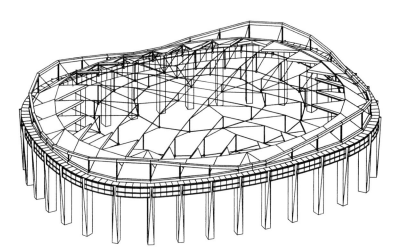

4.13. The hoop dome proposed for Giants Stadium in New Jersey is clad with a retractable membrane that can be (a) opened or (b) closed in one hour. In an original scheme, the cable-and-strut trusses do not converge to a central tension ring; rather, the main trusses span the diagonal of the roughly rectangular plan. Geiger Engineers, engineer; HOK Architects, architect. (Drawings courtesy Geiger Engineers.)

a

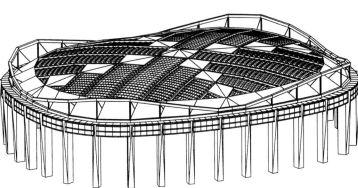

b

If designing deployable structures can increase safety by minimizing or eliminating the need for scaffolding, it can also reduce costs; at times the largest single cost of a structure is the rental, transportation, assembly, and disassembly of scaffolding. Saitoh accomplished a wonderfully clever use of scaffolding in the Nihon University Sports Hall, built in 1985. After the end walls and long side walls of the gym were built, scaffolding was erected only at one end (fig. 4.14). A temporary factory was built on top of the scaffolding. There the roof was assembled in sections, complete with lighting and painting. Then the roof was slid over the side walls like a kimono cloth being pulled across the work area of a loom. The completed roof weighs 1,000 tons, but only 30–40 tons of pulling force was needed to slide the roof. The entire span of 85 meters was built with a small section of scaffolding.

So far we have looked at permanent structures that were preassembled and then deployed on site, but to some architects, deployable structures need not be permanent. Todd Dalland and Nicholas Goldsmith, of FTL Architects, have designed itinerant buildings on trucks. The $3.5 million Carlos Moseley Music Pavilion in New York travels regularly between sixteen park locations in the five boroughs, carried in five trucks that pass over bridges and along city streets (plate 35). The tractor trailer beds are limited to cargoes 13 feet high and 45 feet long, yet their cargo deploys in six hours to become a 40-by-78-foot stage covered by a 68-foot-high A-frame truss that supports an acoustical membrane made of PVC-coated polyester. Upon arrival three trucks back up to form the points of a triangle (fig. 4.15). To set up the stage, large-pad feet are lowered to the ground to hydraulically level and support the trucks; no scars are left on the lawn, no holes are dug, no turf needs to be replaced. The stage is automatically unfolded by a hydraulic piston. Next the two front A-frame trusses are partially raised so that they can be unhinged to their full 86-foot length and con-

nected together. These front trusses have lighting permanently wired inside them. An ingenious combination of mechanical parts allows the rear truss to act like a crane, lifting all three sections as it unfolds, the front two trusses being anchored by full rotation pivots that allow them to swing into place from fixed positions. The membrane can now be unfolded on the stage and hoisted taut. To save packing space the membrane's edge cable is a pliable synthetic fiber rope rather than a more permanent steel cable; it will likely have to be replaced every two years, or after forty deployments, but the architect thought the tradeoff was satisfactory. For Dalland the music pavilion is just the start; he has developed plans for a similar truck-delivered performance venue that includes covered space for the audience as well as the performers.[15]

The most completely deployable semipermanent structure to date is the Venezuelan Pavilion, built for the Exposition in Seville in 1992 by Waclaw Zalewski, of MIT, and his former student C. Hernández Merchan, now of the Central University of Venezuela (plates 36–37). The Venezuelan government commissioned a building to be built in Venezuela from Venezuelan aluminum, shipped to Seville in two containers, each measuring 3 by 2.8 by 18 meters, erected for the exhibition, and repacked and returned to Venezuela after the exhibition was over. Zalewski designed a folded plane truss that could pack into one container yet deploy into a connected roof and wall, each 18 by 22 meters, in less than a day. The complete structure, formed from 6,475 parts and weighing a total of 10,000 kilograms, with 1,242 square meters of surface area, was assembled in two days.

Unlike the scissor mechanisms of Piñero, Hoberman, or Escrig Pallarés (who served as construction engineer for this project), the one designed by Zalewski is an accordion-fold mechanism in which the double-layer plane truss is pleated and hinged (fig. 4.16). The key to the

22. Compression members do not touch in Kenneth Snelson's 60-foot-tall Needle Tower, completed in 1968. (Collection of the Hirshhorn Museum. Photo: Kenneth Snelson.)

23. In René Motro's prototype of a double-layer, double-curvature tensegrity system, continuous cables join the nodes. (Photo: René Motro.)

24. The delicacy of Saitoh's Amagi Dome, completed in 1991, is emphasized by red wooden struts inside the dome and the absence of catwalks on the hoop cables. (Photo courtesy Masao Saitoh.)

25. The Redbird Arena at Illinois State University, shown under construction without membrane or catwalks, is an elliptical-plan gymnasium completed in 1989. The structure is already stable at this point in its construction yet is made with little material. David Geiger and associates, engineers; CRSS of Houston, architect; Birdair, roof fabricator and installer. (Photo courtesy Geiger Engineers.)

26. The nontriangulated radial trusses and the tilted dome are visible in this construction photo of the Suncoast Dome in St. Petersburg, completed in 1988. David Geiger, engineer; Hellmuth, Obata and Kassabaum, architect; Birdair, fabricator and installer of the tensegrity roof. (Photo: Air Innovations, Tampa, Florida.)

27. A triangulated tensegrity design with hypar (hyperbolic paraboloid) panels was chosen for Atlanta's Georgia Dome, completed in 1992. Matthys Levy and others at Weidlinger Associates, engineers; Heery Architects and Engineers, Rosser Fabrap International, and Thompson, Ventulett, Stainback and Associates, architects; Birdair, roof fabricator and installer. (Photo: Robert Reck, courtesy Birdair.)

28. This detail of the triangulated tensegrity roof of the Georgia Dome shows the welded plate nodes. (Photo: Robert Reck, courtesy Birdair.)

29. The walls of Kobe's World Memorial Hall, completed in 1985, are hinged in three places so that the roof can be built on the ground and then lifted into place—an example of the Pantadome system. Mamoru Kawaguchi, engineer; Mitsumune, architect. (Photo courtesy Mamoru Kawaguchi.)

30. The Palau Sant Jordi in Barcelona is a Pantadome, built on the ground, then erected in ten days. Mamoru Kawaguchi, engineer; Arata Isozaki, architect; Orona Corporation, contractor. (Photo courtesy Mamoru Kawaguchi.)

31. The folds in the roof of the Palau Sant Jordi are glazed to reveal the history of the erection process. (Photo courtesy Mamoru Kawaguchi.)

32. The wood and fiberglass dome in Izumo, Japan, completed in 1992, was built on the ground. Masao Saitoh and engineers from the Kajima Corporation, engineers. (Photo courtesy Masao Saitoh.)

33. Once assembled on the ground, the Izumo dome was erected by being pulled up a temporary center post. (Photo courtesy Masao Saitoh.)

34. At night the Izumo dome becomes a giant lantern. (Photo courtesy Masao Saitoh.)

35. The Carlos Moseley Music Pavilion, built in 1991, comes to a New York City park on trucks and is deployed in six hours. Nicholas Goldsmith and associates, FTL Architects, designers. (Photo: Jeff Goldberg, Esto, courtesy FTL Architects.)

36. The Venezuelan Pavilion at the 1992 Exposition in Seville is an accordion truss that arrived from Venezuela in two cargo containers. The main structure was erected in less than a day. Waclaw Zalewski and C. Hernández Merchan, engineers and designers. (Photo courtesy Waclaw Zalewski.)

37. To complete the Venezuelan Pavilion, thin panels were attached to the accordion truss. (Photo courtesy Waclaw Zalewski.)

4.14. Masao Saitoh built a factory atop the scaffolding at one end of the Nihon University Sports Hall to manufacture the hall roof. As sections of the roof were completed, they were pulled across the span. (Photos courtesy Masao Saitoh.)

4.15. To erect FTL's Carlos Moseley Pavilion (see plate 35), the trucks back into position and unfold the trusses attached to their beds. The tripod formed by the trusses is then raised to support a membrane. (Photos: Jeff Goldberg, Esto, courtesy FTL Architects.)

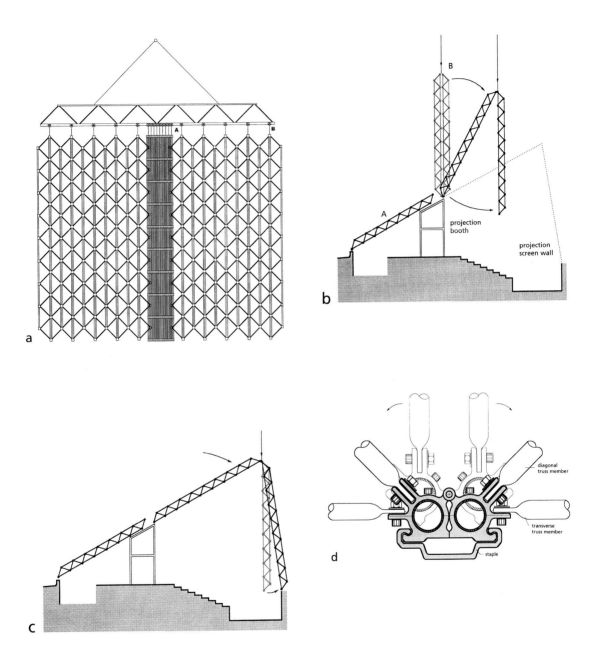

4.16. The main structure of the Venezuelan Pavilion for the 1992 Exposition in Seville, built by Waclaw Zalewski and C. Hernández Merchan, can be assembled in less than a day. (a) It is made from an accordion truss that is pulled open along a suspended rail. (b, c) When pulled open, the accordion truss is attached to the projection booth and swung into position. (d) A staple secures the accordion hinge in its open position. (Drawings courtesy Waclaw Zalewski.)

system is the manufacture of strong, lightweight hinge elements at a reasonable cost, and this was accomplished by the extrusion of long aluminum sections that could be cut and notched to be half hinges. (Such complicated sections perhaps could not have been cast or extruded in steel—certainly not at a competitive price.) When pinned together, the hinges are connected by aluminum rods and become the nodes of a folding system. At first sight, one might assume that the rods in the hinged lattice structure must pivot in two directions as the accordion unfolds. But, as making an accordion fold with a piece of paper shows, long, flat pleats of paper, on which any lattice pattern can be drawn, unfold along the paper hinge. The truss, we see, can be completely assembled and folded at the factory. The hinges are designed with flanges that, when a hinge is fully opened, can be spanned by a "staple" that locks the hinge in an open position; these staples hold the entire structure rigid, although the plate covering and some extra rods also help stabilize the folds.[16]

The accordion-fold roof and walls are deployed in an elegant way. First note, however, that the designers have saved themselves quite a bit of trouble by planning that almost half the structure is excavation. The pavilion is a film theater, and the floor of the theater and the support for the seating are cut into ground. The designers need concern themselves only with a roof and a long projection wall, which must be clear of columns. The roof is in two sections, a smaller section A and a larger section B; the larger section has the projection screen wall hinged to it. The tips of the accordion folds are on rollers, which are threaded on a rail. When the rail is raised by two cranes, the accordion folds can easily be pulled open (fig. 4.17). Section A is lifted by crane and attached to its pivot point; then it is lowered onto its support above the projection booth. Section B is raised on a rail, separated into two halves—the roof section and the

projection screen wall—then opened along its accordion folds. Once the sections have been opened, and the staples slipped over the hinges and bolted in place, panels can be bolted over the framework. It was not possible for the panels to be attached at the factory, and therefore some assembly is required after the structure has been deployed.[17] Still, the panels—which are sandwiches of polyester resin, rigid polyethylene foam, and galvanized steel—were made in Venezuela, came in one of the two containers, and were quickly installed without requiring any trimming on site.

Powerful economic and humanitarian forces are motivating further use of deployable structures. The term describes a whole continuum, from structures that deploy in outer space without human intervention, to large buildings on earth that are constructed without "falsework," as scaffolding is appropriately called. A variety of strategies are being studied: pantograph mechanisms, accordion folds, telescoping struts, cable-drawn tensegrity systems, and inflation systems. Because we have the capability for deployment and because deployment is manifestly superior to traditional construction methods, it is bound to become as basic to architectural design as the concepts of functional use, efficient use of material, and comfort; clients and occupants will demand that the construction of their buildings be as rational as the finished design. The rationality of deployment will be necessary for the structure to be aesthetically complete.

a

b

c

4.17. A sequence of construction photos shows the accordion truss of the Venezuelan Pavilion (a) folded, (b) suspended and being pulled open, and (c) in its fixed position. (Photos courtesy Waclaw Zalewski.)

# 5

# Shells

Classical domes have a thickness-to-radius ratio of 1:50; eggshells can have a thickness-to-radius ratio of 1:100; modern concrete shell domes can be built to the astounding ratio of 1:800.[1] Constructed with small quantities of simple, inexpensive, low-tech concrete and wire mesh, these structures are safe as well as beautiful. With a faith in geometry that the ancient Pythagoreans would have appreciated, practitioners have come to the counterintuitive realization that the strength of shells results from their shape, not their mass: in a structural sense they embody—in concrete—the famous architectural dictum "Less is more."

Heinz Isler, a Swiss engineer who in the course of thirty-five years has built more than 1,500 thin-shell concrete domes (box), has synthesized his experience into an equation. He says that he depends on this equation and uses it each time he builds. Yet at least two of the terms are fudge factors—judgment calls and approximations based on educated intuition—which shows that the engineering of thin shells is still as much art as it is science. Here is his formula:

$$P_k = \frac{C}{\alpha \cdot \beta \cdot \gamma} \cdot E \cdot \left(\tfrac{t}{r}\right)^x \geq 5 \cdot P_{eff}$$

It states that the critical buckling load ($P_k$) is equal to a constant ($C$) times the modulus of elasticity ($E$) of the concrete (a very large number) times the ratio, raised to a power, of the

thickness of the shell ($t$) divided by the radius of the shell ($r$) (actually the median of the two radii of curvature), which defines the curvature of the shell. This ratio will always be a very small number. The constant $C$ is the product of three numbers: $\alpha$, unknown at first, is the result of the computation and must be solved between 0.2 and 1.2; $\beta$ is a long-studied and well-known margin-of-error factor due to inaccuracies in the shape, about 0.3; and $\gamma$ is a number, learned from experience with models or previous structures, that is specific to each shape of the shell and, in the case of a sphere, is equal to 1. Most powerful is $x$, the exponent, which is also dependent on the specific shape and has been learned and catalogued by Isler from experience; its value ranges from 3 for a cylinder to 2 for a sphere. For a stable shell the critical buckling load must greater than or equal to an effective load, $P_{eff}$ (say, of snow), times a safety factor, in Isler's case a factor of 3.

Even though the values of some of these variables are part of Isler's "private compass," as he calls it, there is still much to learn from the equation. One lesson for architects that Isler points out is that spherical parts of a shell have approximately thirty times the buckling resistance of cylindrical ones. A second lesson concerns the sensitivity of shells to their height and degree of curvature. In a traditional shell the ratio of the height to the diagonal of the plan is about 1:10. In a dome that steeply curved, the concrete can still be easily applied to the form-work (the temporary structure that is the mold for the concrete). When the height and steepness increase, so that the ratio goes from 1:10 to 1:7, the shell becomes twice as strong, because that smaller radius of curvature is squared ($10 \times 10 = 100$; $7 \times 7 = 49$) in the $(t/r)^x$ term of the formula. In general, Isler makes shells that are higher than other engineers', and he avoids cylinders like the plague.[2]

The appeal of shells is that they are strong, and Isler's "destruction tests" of two shells in Uster, Switzerland, dramatically confirm that strength. In 1981 the connected shells—each approximately 20 meters square with a large central skylight and set on four columns—needed to be demolished to make room for another structure. Isler took the opportunity to test the strength of his shells. First he overloaded the edge beam of one shell, then added weight to the rim of the skylight and punched six holes, placed symmetrically around the skylight, at the meridian of maximum curvature of the shell—right where one could imagine the center of the shell collapsing. Next, with a crane and a wrecking ball he simulated a meteorite attack, making a large hole midway between a corner post and the skylight. All this assault notwithstanding, the shell could probably still have passed inspection, as there seemed to be no change in its shape or cracks in its surface.

On the other shell, Isler simulated the subsidence of one of the columns, removing 20 centimeters from the bottom (fig. 5.1). He proceeded to remove 50 centimeters, 1 meter, 2 meters, and finally the entire 4-meter column. The shell now had major longitudinal cracks from the site of the removed column to the central skylight and cracks at the edge where the two shells met. The shell had not collapsed, however. Indeed, the shape of the shell was still intact when two columns were removed and one whole edge beam was resting on the ground. Isler notes that

## Heinz Isler

Heinz Isler has the reputation of being the only engineer alive who can scale up a shell model to a full-size building with the accuracy needed to make a stable structure. But he also has a fanciful and playful imagination, searching for new forms by spraying water on thin cloth on cold Zurich nights: he makes frozen tent shapes; hollow, crystal-clear ice spheres supported by art deco ooze; and mathematically pure hypars in ghostly moonscapes. Perhaps some great discovery still awaits him, but like his delightful domes, Isler shows no signs of stress about it. Unusually, Isler is not a professor at a university. He just likes to make things, and, like Félix Candela, he is the builder as well as the architect and engineer of his domes. He has created other shells that are pure sculpture. One of his half-dozen or so sculptures, the largest is the 9-meter-high *Monument* in Hafen von Pully, Switzerland, made in 1978.

5.1. In a demolition experiment, although Heinz Isler (a) removed one of the four corner pillars supporting the thin concrete shell, (b) removed a second pillar, and finally (c) removed a third, the shell remained intact. (d) The crushed shell provided remarkably little rubble to remove. (Photo courtesy Heinz Isler.)

the occupants of the shell would survive even if the shell was supported on only one column.

When the material for these two shells was pulverized, in only one and a half hours, it could be removed in half a day. A very small amount of concrete had withstood destruction because its shape made it strong. There has been another demonstration of the strength of shells, at an

automobile and truck repair plant in Nesslau that was built as a series of 30-meter shells. Although a 10-ton rolling crane was installed twenty-five years ago, supported only by the beam-reinforced shell edges, the shell remains unaffected (fig. 5.2).[3]

As Isler notes, the correct curvature in a shell results in minimum bending, which, in

5.2. This 10-ton rolling crane is supported by beam-reinforced shell edges. (Photo courtesy Heinz Isler.)

turn, results in minimum cracking, thus preventing water from penetrating the shell and corroding the metal reinforcing rod or mesh inside the concrete. Quality control in construction is still necessary. Isler usually uses 325 kilograms of concrete per cubic meter, giving the proper viscosity for careful working even on steep areas. All parts of the shell are vibrated to remove air pockets. The shells are so smoothly finished that "gas infiltration is practically stopped and carbonation is limited to the outer 2mm to 6mm." The result is an appealing gray surface that needs no maintenance and that does not further degrade even if lichen and mosses grow on its surface. Isler uses two layers of reinforcement and generally likes to keep the thickness in the 5-centimeter vicinity. He says that his shells are not the thinnest possible, even though their common thickness-to-radius ratio of 1:200 makes them proportionally twice as thin as eggshells, nor are his shells made with the newest concretes. They are, however, devoid of ribs and "give no headaches to their owners."[4]

Isler is adamant about finding the shapes for his shells by experimenting with physical models, as opposed to selecting a shape defined by the geometry of mathematical formulas. (With such mathematically defined surfaces as hypars—hyperbolic paraboloids—any point on

the shell can be compared with its ideal mathematical point, making it easier to check the accuracy of the shell construction.) Isler claims that forms derived from physical experiment are stronger than those derived from formulas because they are forms of pure compression, with no tension or bending forces to crack the concrete. Soap bubbles, for example, are forms of pure tension, for only the surface tension in the soapy water holds the shape against the outward pressure of the air inside the bubble. A soap bubble on a frame is, then, as close to a pure membrane shape as possible. Rising out of a square frame, it has a free shape not easily modeled by mathematics. Made out of concrete, that shape is one of pure compression, because the deadweight of the concrete is the inverse of the outward air pressure in the bubble: only

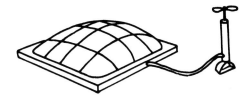

5.3. To discover a shell shape by physical experiment, Isler makes a bubble to measure by clamping down and inflating a sheet of rubber. (Drawing courtesy Heinz Isler.)

compression holds the shape together, not tension or bending stiffness. To find the appropriate shapes for his domes, Isler clamps rubber sheets in the desired floor plan, inflates these rubber "bubbles," and measures the height of the surface above the plan (fig. 5.3).

With only the most meticulous care can Isler determine the height of the model at every point of the plan, and with only the most precise carpentry can the surface be replicated in formwork. An error of curvature of merely a few centimeters can greatly weaken such a shell, and because the shell may be fifty times as large as the model, the measurement tolerance for the model must be a tiny 0.1 millimeter.[5] The measurements are so subtle that even Isler's body heat can change the shape; once, standing over the inflated rubber, he warmed the trapped air, which expanded and raised the surface by 0.1 millimeter. He had to repeat the measurements while encased in winter coat, hat, and mittens.

Besides using soap, then rubber bubbles to find forms, Isler freezes hanging membranes in place (fig. 5.4). The plan, elevations, and window spans are chosen by the architect (in many of Isler's best shells, this is Michael Baltz), and then a fabric shape is cut by trial and error. The liquid load—either water or resin—stretches the membrane. Repeated attempts are made to find the

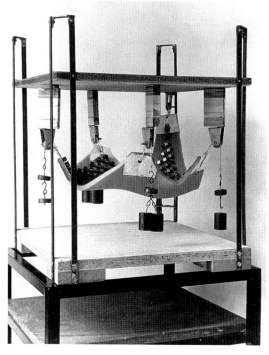

5.5. When heated and weighted, acrylic plastic sags into shapes that can be used for concrete shells. (Photo courtesy Oscar Andrés and Néstor Ortega.)

smooth surface that meets all requirements. Even small models no longer than an arm provide accurate shapes that can be scaled up to buildings. Once found, the hanging shape is repeated in other models for statical testing (that is, testing for the force of weight). By adjusting the shape and then retesting, improvements in load capacity of up to 30 percent can be gained with the same thickness of shell and the same amount of materials.[6] Optimization to such a degree—30 percent—is a serious challenge to attempts at computer enhancements of shell shapes.

A third method of building physical models for shells is to heat acrylic sheets, like Plexiglas, under loads (fig. 5.5). Two physical facts make such an approach appealing: the elastic behavior of acrylic sheets is similar to that of concrete, and equal loads per unit area give equal stresses

5.4. Frozen hanging membranes also provide Isler with shapes for thin-shell buildings. (Photo courtesy Heinz Isler.)

in both the model and the real object.[7] Oscar A. Andrés, of the National University of the South in Argentina, and Néstor F. Ortega have described the experimental designs that they have created with acrylic in two *Proceedings* of conferences of the International Association for Shell and Space Structures (IASS 1991, 1994). First, acrylic plates originally 300 millimeters on a side and 1 millimeter thick are cut into various shapes, including a symmetrical hexagonal star and various free-form shapes. To discover the pure compression shape, a "loading carpet" is prepared: a polyester sheet is cut in the same shapes, then small pieces of iron are attached at regular intervals. For such a thin material, loads of 150 kilogram per square meter are chosen, making the weight roughly comparable to that of a thin concrete shell. The loading carpet is placed on an acrylic plate, and the plate is counterbalanced by weights over pulleys attached to the eventual "feet" of the shell. The entire apparatus is placed in an oven with an even heat of 125 degrees centigrade (257 degrees Fahrenheit) for three-quarters of an hour. When heated, the acrylic deforms until it reaches a new equilibrium. "Since the model was formed when the plastic material had a very low (or negligible) bending stiffness, due to heat action, it will have a minimum bending behavior for the designing load"; that is, that the shell should be purely in compression when inverted and made of concrete. Andrés and his colleagues have made computer analyses of the stresses in shapes generated this way and compared them with pure membrane surfaces generated by mathematics in the same shape. They have found that the physical model comes very close to reproducing the ideal surface, with generally less than 2 percent difference in their height, and that the physical and ideal models behaved similarly in computer tests.[8]

Initially, experts differed on whether there was any useful purpose in computer analysis of shells or in attempts at shape optimization with computers. Shells were first analyzed as membranes (substituting tension for compression), but then it became obvious that edge beams and flat areas where two shells were joined introduced bending stresses in the shell that were resisted by the bending stiffness of the reinforced concrete.[9] Membrane analysis was considered incomplete at best. But now that shells can be made with thin free edges and with shapes generated by accurate physical experiment, membrane analysis may be more relevant, especially in its state-of-the-art form.

Alex Scordelis, of the University of California, Berkeley, has been developing computer programs to analyze thin-shell roofs since 1960. Scordelis and his coworkers have used membrane theory modified to include bending effect, together with finite element and finite strip analysis (which sum over large numbers of discrete sections) and, since the early 1970s, nonlinear, time-dependent analysis, which continually feeds back into the program the developing shape of the shell. Scordelis's programs trace the "complete structural response of these structures throughout their service load history and under increasing loads up to ultimate failure" and gives "joint displacements, internal strains and stresses in the concrete, and crack patterns." Scordelis's most recent programs even model for such real-life effects as "load history; temperature history, creep, shrinkage, and aging of the concrete; and other prestress losses due to anchor slip, friction, and relaxation."[10] Such complex computer analyses are needed in the design of such critical structures as off-shore drilling platforms, where huge, hollow underwater concrete shells are used to float the platforms. The analyses are also useful to calibrate simpler programs.

John Abel, professor of civil engineering at Cornell University, and his coworkers have developed interactive computer programs for designing shells. The power and flexibility of the programs comes from being topology based: stored structures are thought of as being composed of elements with neighbors rather than being components with coordinates. These topology-based computer models are easily modified. Geometric models of increasing detail are made from the internal topological models for display, general structural analysis, or finite element analysis. The goal is interactive design coupled with engineering analysis readout, so that a user can obtain moment-by-moment knowledge of successive versions of a shell and develop an intuitive sense of structure.

Perhaps the greatest value of accurate computer analysis of shells is the possibility that it provides for automatic computer optimization of shape and supporting ribs. Ekkehard Ramm, of the University of Stuttgart, has developed two methods by which computers can be used to optimize shells: shape optimization and topology optimization. The first is an extrapolation of the force-density method for finding the best placements of nodes in a prestressed cable structure; that is, nodes are mathematically slid around an idealized cable net (the length and the angles of the cable segments are varied) until a balance is found. For shells the goal is to find shapes as free

of tension and bending forces as possible, so nodes are free to move up and down and the shell can become thinner in the process until the strain energy is minimized. The program has many parameters; generally the total material is held constant, and loads are added to obtain a more realistic optimization. Program runs usually raise the height of intuitively chosen free-form shells and thin the shells. Negative curvature is usually introduced at the free edges, allowing them to gracefully swoop up (fig. 5.6).[11]

In Ramm's second method, topology optimization, the shell is imagined to be made up of discrete cells, or microholes, each surrounded by a thick border (fig. 5.7). After the computer run, the walls of the border are either thick, meaning there is material at that point, or vanishingly thin, meaning that the material has been mentally removed. With the simulation of force, microholes expand or close in the computer model and aggregate to form patterns. Although the strain energy may generally follow expected paths, a lacy structure can evolve, with holes and delicate tracery. Such topological computer simulations show where supporting ribs would be most effective, where the shell thickness could be reduced,

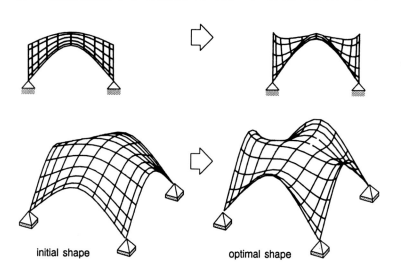

5.6. Ekkehard Ramm's computer program optimizes a shell shape by raising the edges and increasing the curvature. (Drawing courtesy Ekkehard Ramm.)

initial shape                    optimal shape

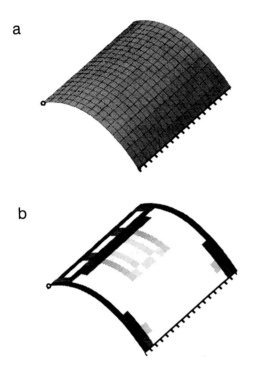

a

b

5.7. Here are (a) a shell shape and (b) the result of Ramm's microhole computer analysis. Dark shading shows where the shell should be thickened; light shading, where it can be thinned. (Drawings courtesy Ekkehard Ramm.)

line station on the Bern-Zurich highway (1968) and his swimming pool in Lugano (1972) were made with such flexible beams (plates 38–39). These beams can be not only reused but reconfigured, making them the most efficient components of formwork over the long run. Inflated fabrics are a second system with a high initial cost but with the possibility of many reuses. Smaller shell buildings can be made by spraying concrete (or another material) on inflated structures. Isler estimates that such formwork balloons could be used over fifty times. Pneumatic formwork is not associated with his most elegant shell shapes, however. Isler has also experimented with molded earth forms. With this method, components of shells are cast on the same sculpted mound of earth and then crane-lifted into place.

Beams of laminated timber can be reused fifteen to twenty times. The beams cannot change shape, so they can be reused only when their particular shell shape is reused. With proper varnish and storage, however, they can last many years. Isler especially likes this method because the beams are lightweight and require the fewest labor-hours for placement and removal.[14] An average assembly time for a 10-by-10-meter shell is only ten days. Laminated beams have been used for shells as large as 60 by 60 meters in size. The beautiful Garden Center in Camorino, Switzerland, was built by this method in 1973 (fig. 5.8). For free-form single-use shells, wooden boards can be cut curved for the formwork. Single-use cut-board formwork was used, for example, to make the 28-by-42-meter shell for an open-air theater, built in Grötzingen in 1977, designed with Michael Baltz (fig. 5.9).

One appealing and clever use of formwork is to make the final curved surface out of insulating material, cast the concrete on that insulating material, and then leave the material in place, removing only the beams and posts. Isler has discovered that for most uses condensation is not a problem. Moisture can expire through the thin

or where holes and skylights would have the least structural impact.[12] The patterns open up shell design and allow for greater visual richness in the architecture.

Formwork, the temporary mold, is the big concern with shells. Traditionally it was thought that formwork was 50 percent of the cost of a shell. Isler made his reputation in 1959 by claiming that formwork could cost only 20 percent of the construction budget. The savings were achieved primarily by reusing parts or all of the formwork. In 1984 he catalogued these techniques.[13] Flexible beams are trusses with adjustable diagonals; they can be bent to any desired curvature. Once adjusted, they are bolted rigid and can support a form. Both his BP gaso-

5.8. Isler's Garden Center in Camorino, Switzerland, was built with reused laminated timber beams for the form-work. (Photo courtesy Heinz Isler.)

5.9. The beautiful free-form shell for the Open Air Theater in Grötzingen, near Stuttgart, was designed by Isler and Michael Baltz. (Photo courtesy Heinz Isler.)

concrete, and the insulating material can gradually expel the rest. Examples of this construction technique have been in existence since 1955 without damage to either the concrete shell or the insulating boards.[15]

Vladimir Shugaev and his colleagues at the Research Institute for Concrete and Reinforced Concrete in Moscow have bent flat concrete slabs in place to make curved shells, removing the need for formwork altogether. In one example of this technique, reinforced concrete slabs are cast measuring 2.55 by 9 meters in width and length and 40 millimeters in thickness. After the slabs are completely matured, they are placed end to end and bent over supporting ribs. Steel flanges cast into the edges of the slabs are welded together, and the seams are filled with fresh concrete. Only limited curvature is possible with this method, but prestressing the slabs allows increased curvature without cracking the concrete. Structures with 24-meter spans have been assembled.

A second method studied in Moscow is the bending of flat concrete plates when the concrete is still fresh. This is accomplished by laying a slab on an inflated membrane form, by winding the fresh slab around a rigid curved core, or by allowing the plate to sag under its own weight using flexible formwork. The last method has been found to be the most useful, resulting in the fewest cracks (fig. 5.10). Steel fiber reinforcement as opposed to wire mesh reinforcement improves this method, for the wire mesh can foul in bending and cause cracking. Rhomb-shaped curved elements can be made accurately and cheaply, then assembled in a great variety of domes and vaults, including structures based on accordion-fold designs, the high-frequency subdivision of polyhedra, and labyrinths with complex curvature. Rhombs 20–25 millimeters thin and up to 30 meters from corner to corner across the long diagonal have been proposed, and quarter-scale prototypes have undergone laboratory testing. The unmistakable benefit of Shugaev's

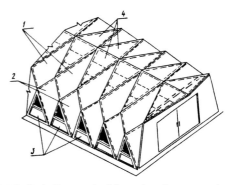

5.10. Vladimir Shugaev's philosophy of mass-producing and assembling many shell sections could revitalize shell architecture. (Drawing from Shugaev 1994, 876.)

methods is mass-produced shell segments. This ambitious new approach could well revitalize the architecture of shell structures by increasing the variety of possible forms.

The field does need revitalizing. Only one member of the International Association for Shell and Space Structures (Isler) now makes shells, and only a few members study them. Oh, plenty of shells are pumped out for industrial purposes, but no avant-garde architect or research engineer would want to report about that at an IASS meeting. Jörg Schlaich, himself a lapsed shellmaker, has even written an article in the IASS *Bulletin* entitled "Do Concrete Shells Have a Future?"[16] But he fails to answer the question that he really means to ask: Should there be a future for shells?

All the reasons usually cited for abandoning shell architecture turn out to be false. Among others, David Billington, an engineering professor at Princeton, has noted that Félix Candela developed his marvelous shells in Mexico, which in the 1950s had inexpensive labor to build formwork, along with relaxed building codes, while materials other than concrete were relatively expensive (box).[17] But concrete is still plentiful and cheap; the cost of formwork can be reduced by designing reusable formwork and taking advantage of other techniques; and the alterna-

## Spanish Shells

The architect Antonio Gaudí began the tradition of shell structures in Spain in the early 1900s. He made inverted funicular models of his vaults (strings supported on both ends and pulled taut are called funiculars) and loaded them with weights proportional to the deadweight, compressive loads of the buildings. This natural form-finding method revolutionized thinking about architectural shapes. Gaudí also looked to the natural world—turtle shells, plant stems and leaves, even fish—and was perhaps the first to see that these streamlined and complexly curved shapes spoke of efficient structure as well as decoration. Early in the 1900s, Gaudí first made saddle-shaped (hyperbolic paraboloid) roofs; he admired the practicality of the straight-line generation and associated the three straight-line generators of the curved shape with the Holy Trinity. (Two crossed lines rotated around a central axis make a rotational hyperboloid. This means that formwork for hypars can be built up with straight lines, which greatly facilitates the building of formwork.) His Schools of the Sagrada Familia Church, built in Barcelona in 1909 and made of layers of overlapping tiles and tar paper, still stands.

Eduardo Torroja, a Madrid engineer and founder of the IASS, built astoundingly strong cast-concrete shells in the 1930s. The often-mentioned Zarzuela Hippodrome roof is a series of hyperbolic vaults that cantilevers out 42 feet and has a thickness of only 2 inches at the free end. The structure looks modern and daring even today. Torroja was a highly respected theorist and writer and has become the model for the practicing engineers who are also academics who have contributed so much to the built environment.

Félix Candela, besides being an architect, was an athlete, revolutionary, and expatriate. He was a Spanish national champion skier and captain of a national champion rugby team. He fought against Franco in the Spanish Civil War, and, after a brief internment, fled to Mexico upon Franco's victory. This turn of fate was a boon to thin-shell architecture. Mexico had relaxed building codes, a ready pool of skilled labor to build formwork, and an appreciation for the economy of concrete. Candela's brother even won a large lottery prize and could finance some of his early studies and projects. Candela's later shells are astonishingly thin. His Cosmic Ray Pavilion, for example, built near Mexico City in 1951, is 1.5 centimeters (0.59 inches) thick over a span of 10.75 meters (35.4 feet). Candela, who now lives in Madrid, has not made shells for several decades.

tives to shells, such as spaceframes, with their myriad node connections, are labor intensive as well as material intensive. The craft-versus-science argument is probably also false. It in no way denigrates Isler's achievements in model-making and quality control to point out that advanced computer analysis and computer optimization make it possible for others to make stable, elegant thin shells. Some complain that shells are suited only for one-story buildings and that the ceilings in these buildings cannot hide mechanical systems, but the same can be said of membrane structures. Finally, the Sydney Opera House fiasco, often adduced as the coup de grâce for thin-shell structures because the building was so late and so much over budget, cannot be enough to kill off a whole architectural style, no matter how exasperating it was for all concerned; in fact, the structure is so striking and memorable that it has become an icon for Sydney all over the world: we could say that it has been a success after all.[18]

What is the real reason for the premature demise of shells? I believe we can blame a knee-jerk minimalism still popular among engineers but rightfully abandoned by almost everyone else—an assumption that only efficiency and economy are aesthetic, or that they are aesthetic in only one (namely, minimalist) way. Proponents and apologists for shells are not willing to dissociate the building technology from the cultural imagery with which it has temporarily become identified, thus restricting the possible applications of shells in the minds of architects.

Shells are too good an idea to restrict to a minimalist aesthetic, which, after all, is just another artistic proposition formulated by humans at a particular moment in cultural history, now long past. The shellmaker Antonio Gaudí was not a minimalist. The economy of mass, thinness, gracefulness, and innate strength of double curvature can have a different architectural image: convoluted, multiply connected, and fluid. Rather than study a single soap bubble,

38. This BP gas station on the Bern-Zurich highway was made with reusable, flexible beams. (Photo courtesy Heinz Isler.)

39. Isler's shell interiors are filled with light from high side walls and large skylights, as with this swimming pool in Aarepark, Switzerland. Heinz Isler, engineer; Gross, Hermann and Meier, architect. (Photo courtesy Heinz Isler.)

40. Hybrid systems were used for a large, low-profile vault in Sakata, in the high snow region of Yamagata prefecture, Japan. The roof flattens out automatically when accommodating snow loads. Masao Saitoh and Kozo Keikaku, engineers; Taniguchi and Associates, architect. (Photo courtesy Masao Saitoh.)

41. From the inside, the roof of the Sakata gym seems to float above the walls. The interior of the gym is visually lightweight because the fittings are delicate and because the supporting structure is on the exterior. (Photo courtesy Masao Saitoh.)

42. A cable net is strung under the glass of a thin-mullion grid dome over a swimming pool in Neckarsulm. The dome was erected and glazed within two months. Jörg Schlaich, engineer. (Photo courtesy Jörg Schlaich.)

43. Schlaich's transparent vault over the Hamburg City Historical Museum is strengthened by a cable net diagonal to the glass grid and by radiating cable spokes. (Photo courtesy Jörg Schlaich.)

44. A quasicrystal sculpture (1994) for the Center for Art, Science, and Technology at Denmark's Technical University. Tony Robbin, artist; Erik Reitzel, engineer; RCB Precision of Mount Vernon, New York, fabricator. (Photo: Poul Ib Henriksen.)

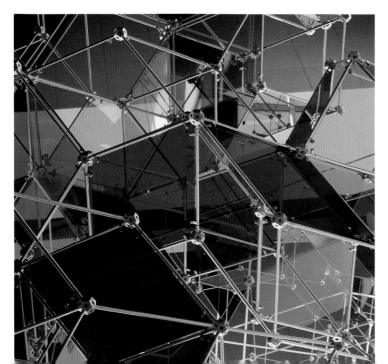

45. A detail of the quasicrystal sculpture shows how standard parts generate a nonrepeating pattern in three-dimensional space with visual richness and subtle organization. (Photo: Poul Ib Henriksen.)

46. The dramatic glass walls of the Kempinski Hotel in Munich are supported by cable stays. Jörg Schlaich, engineer; Helmut Jahn, architect. (Photo courtesy Jörg Schlaich.)

47. The cylindrical glass wall in the Channel Four Building in London is kept in plumb by an enveloping hyperbolic cable net. Ove Arup and Partners, engineer; Richard Rogers Partnership, architect. (Photo: Peter Mackinven, courtesy Ove Arup and Partners.)

48. Cable stays allow the glass walls of Amsterdam's Glass Music Hall, completed in 1989, to be hung from the roof. Mick Eekhout, Octatube, engineer and fabricator; Pieter Zaanen, architect. (Photo courtesy Mick Eekhout.)

5.11. Isler's basic shell shape, derived by physical experiment and used over and over again, is wonderfully delicate. (Photo courtesy Heinz Isler.)

engineers can look at fractal collections of self-similar soap bubbles for inspiration, and shells could also be made using the new computer-driven mathematics of minimal surfaces and labyrinths. Designers of spaces that people inhabit, engineers as well as artists and architects, owe it to their audience to make the built environment at least as vital as the conceptual one. As we have seen, Isler's buildings rest on the ground with the lightness of a crisp, new-fallen autumn leaf (fig. 5.11). It is a failure of imagination on the part of architects and engineers—not an intrinsic limitation of shells—that more complicated shell structures do not also kiss the earth.

# Hybrids

Separate structural systems are well understood; not so well studied is how they can be combined in hybrids. As with plants, good hybrid building systems are not genetic monsters but sly superimpositions of capabilities. Hybrid buildings subtly alternate between two intertwined structural systems, one for normal loads and another that can respond to new circumstances with latent strength.

In the Sakata gym, built in the high snow region of Yamagata prefecture in 1991–92, Masao Saitoh and the architect Taniguchi and Associates solved a complex and difficult loading problem by creating a hybrid structure (plate 40). During the winter, snow loads can be double the self-weight of a roof, yet the site of the gym, a park containing a small art gallery and located in the midst of rice fields, required a flat roof. To support a flat or slightly curved roof that spanned the required 53 meters, a conventional truss would have had to be massive, very deep, visually oppressive, and out of character with the park buildings and setting (plate 41). The solution was to design two structures for the two different loading conditions and allow the building to convert from one to the other, to inhale and exhale with the rhythm of the seasons.

In Saitoh's terminology, the central part of the roof is supported by many beam-and-string systems (fig. 6.1a). In this case, the beam-and-string elements are slightly arched steel beams

end-supported by three struts that are in turn supported by a tensioned steel rope attached to the ends of the beams. Each beam end is supported by a rigid cantilever truss with a roughly triangular overall shape, and this cantilever truss is supported by a hinge joint connecting one vertex to the supporting side wall, so that the truss can rock back and forth. The third vertex of the rigid triangular truss is connected to a back stay, a steel bar outside the building connected to the foundation. The beam-and-string systems are connected to the cantilever trusses by rollers that permit limited horizontal movement.

In the summer, when the load on the roof is the weight of the roof itself, tension in the strings arcs the beams upward, opening a gap between the beams and the triangular trusses and rotating the triangular trusses toward the gym floor, a motion resisted by tension in the back stays. Thus the lateral thrust of the roof is largely balanced by tensile forces, and the supporting walls can be thin and studded with glass because they support only vertical loads. Most of the bearing structure—the back stays and the rocker trusses—is outside the building, so the inside observer sees only a light, floating roof.

During the winter, the weight of snow flattens the arch of the roof, increasing the tension in the strings; the lateral thrust of the increased weight results in the horizontal movement of the rollers until the gap between beam and truss is

b

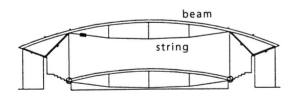

a

6.1. (a) For the roof of the Sakata gym, beam-and-string systems are lightly placed on cantilevering triangular trusses that can pivot to change loading: the roof flattens to support snow loads in winter, then relaxes and arches in summer. (b) The beam-and-string systems were prestressed at ground level before being hoisted into place. (Drawing and photo courtesy Masao Saitoh.)

closed. Closing the gap limits the tension in the strings and locks the beam and the rocker truss into one continuous, rigid, low arch, forced downward by the load of snow. The tension in the back stays is at a minimum.

In other words, the hybrid roof system first functions as a beam, then as a beam-and-string system, and finally as an arch, each part of the system absorbing some of the increasing load. When unloaded, the lightweight roof relaxes into a delicately balanced structure.

Saitoh's building system depends on highly accurate cable lengths for strings that are are 41 meters long. Although hardware exists to tighten the steel ropes once the beam-and-string systems are in place, winching devices like massive turnbuckles are inelegant as well as expensive and further require that all other parts of the roof be designed to accommodate them (there has to be

enough room to not only house but to work the
winches). To set each beam as lightly on the
walls as an archery bow stored in an armory,
Saitoh permitted himself only 2 centimeters of
clearance between the tips of the beams and the
walls of the building (box). The beams were
strung on the ground without the struts
attached, lifted 10 centimeters, and held in this
position for twenty-four hours (fig. 6.1b).
Considerable variation in the sag of the strings
was observed, even though their lengths had
been accurately marked. The sag was adjusted by
turning small nuts on the ends of the strings: the
lengths of steel ropes 41 meters long were
ultimately accurate to a tolerance of 13 millimeters.[1]

To confirm the efficacy of the rollers, Saitoh
analyzed the behavior of the roof with the rollers
and also with hypothetical hinge connections
between the beam-and-string systems and the
cantilever trusses. With the roller connections,
loads increased compression in the beams and
tension in the strings equally; with hinge connections, compression in the beams increased to
four and one-half times the tension in the
strings. With rollers, loads were generally distributed equally among the members of the cantilever truss, whereas with hinges, loads were
less equally distributed. Such studies, as well as
the example of the building itself, are highly suggestive: buildings with moving structural parts,
with structural systems activated when they are
needed and quiescent at other times, can be built
and can be elegant and efficient.[2]

Saitoh modified his concept for a large gymnasium (78 by 112 meters) containing several
swimming pools, which was built in Nagoya in
1992 (fig. 6.2). The shallow spaceframe roof is in
sections with the spherical curvature of large
radii (more than 450 meters). The bowed-in roof
is hinged along the ridge and is attached to the
supporting walls with rollers. Eighteen cables
pull the roof trusses inward and upward, balancing the dead load of the roof. Snow loads of 60

## Masao Saitoh

Poetic metaphors abound in the engineering and architecture of Masao Saitoh's deployable and hybrid structures. When he designs buildings, Saitoh thinks of butterflies in cocoons, bamboo umbrellas, and kimono cloths being woven on a loom. For the Sakata gym, his image was of flying cranes gliding to a landing on a rice field: delicate, elongated flat wings close to the ground, made strong enough for flight by combining different systems.

Saitoh's father was a famous archer, and the son still remembers being impressed by the graceful longbow and the power that it contained in the still moment before the arrow was released. For Saitoh the bow is a symbol of all bending members, and the string, of all tension members. But the arrow holds the argument: without the arrow (the compression member generating flexion and tension), the bow and string have no power and no meaning. When Saitoh wrote his doctoral thesis on tensegrity, the image of the bow occurred naturally. He also discerns the use of a beam-and-string system in such early metal buildings as the Crystal Palace. Tensegrity, then, is for Saitoh the culmination of an old technology reaching back through the beam-and-cable-stay system of the nineteenth century to the bows of medieval Japan.

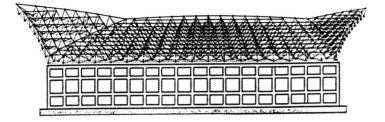

6.2. For a gym in Nagoya, Masao Saitoh uses cables across the span, hinges along the ridge, and rollers along the top of the walls to allow the roof to adjust to different loading conditions. (Drawing courtesy Masao Saitoh.)

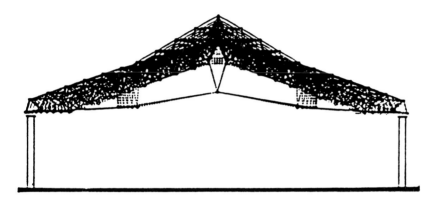

kilograms per square meter flatten the light steel roof and increase the tension in the cables, whereas wind loads primarily create uplift, lessening the tension in the cables. In either wind or snow, the rollers allow the roof to adjust and distribute load, balancing uplift by deadweight and compression in the steel trusses and balancing downward force by tension in the cables.

Jörg Schlaich, of the University of Stuttgart, combines two structural systems, neither of which alone would suffice, to support glass roofs of great airiness and strength. As he explains, glass domes of the nineteenth century were supported by heavy cast-iron beams that converged at the zenith in a trapezoidal grid, congesting the dome at precisely the point it should be most open.[3] Support relied on the bending stiffness in the bars of the cast-iron grid, an inefficient use of materials. The trapezoidal sections of meridians and beams create nonstandard glazing patterns: the panes of glass in each higher course are different from those below. The distributed structure of Fuller's geodesic system avoids this problem but makes three other problems for

designers: the undulating lines of the structure may be distracting; the geodesic pattern accommodates only sections of spheres, which limits the possibilities for design; and the glass panels must be triangles, although they would be much more easily made as quadrilaterals.

Schlaich's solution is to combine a single-layer reticular dome with a cable net to make thin, doubly curved roofs of seemingly square glass panels: the roof looks like a common kitchen strainer paned with glass, as he points out (fig. 6.3).[4] It is startling to ponder the geometry of this common utensil and realize that the surface is curved in two directions, that the metal wires lie in planes, and that the mesh is quadrilateral. When enlarged to become an architectural structure, the system has a major advantage in that all the grid members are identical in length and form. In some shapes, every four nodes of a quadrilateral mesh are on a plane, a feature that is important for glazing, because double-glazed panels can be made up flat and still conform to the surface of the structure (fig. 6.4). Only two sacrifices must be made:

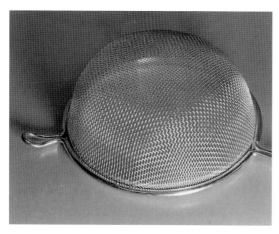

6.3. The kitchen strainer is spherically curved and made up of equal-length quadrilateral openings of relatively few types. (Photo: Tony Robbin.)

6.4. Jörg Schlaich designed nodes that allow mullions to pivot so that only one node type is needed to build a grid-and-glass structure. (Photo courtesy Jörg Schlaich.)

the glass panels are rhombs, not squares (but there are not so many different types of rhombs, and computer-aided design tools can keep track of their types and locations); and the irregular units where the quadrilateral mesh reaches the ground, which are set first during construction, must be very precisely shaped, so that proper curvature is generated as the grid is built up.

Schlaich's kitchen-strainer domes and vaults, with four panels meeting at each vertex, are stable for their self-weight without diagonal bracing but have little resistance to lateral,

dynamic loads, like wind gusts and drifting snow. The resistance to lateral buckling is not provided primarily by the stiffness of the bars but by the tensile, elastic capabilities of the continuous cables running from one point on the perimeter, just under the surface of the dome, to another point on the perimeter, cross-bracing the rhombic bar mesh. These continuous cables make the domes practicable. Because each type of rhomb has two different diagonals, fitting and evenly stressing so many separate elements of cable would be a construction nightmare. But a simple geometric fact—that the two diagonals of all rhombs intersect at right angles—allows the cable diagonals to find their own lengths if strung together with continuous cables. Cables are set in pairs so that each can be thin; light rays bending around the thin cables make them all but invisible to those under the roof. The uncut cables can be coated at the factory, and consequently they are well protected from corrosion. The cable net is slung underneath the single-layer quadrilateral grid and given an initial prestress. Final stressing is simply and elegantly accomplished by clamping the cables 5 millimeters closer to the metal bars of the grid. Thus, the single-layer grid holds the cable net up and stressed, and the cable net triangulates and compresses the quadrilateral grid. The compressive grid resists downward loads, and the tensile cable net catches dynamic loads.

For a swimming pool in Neckarsulm, Schlaich built a spherical dome with a diameter of 16.4 meters and a maximum height of 5.75 meters (plate 42; fig. 6.5). Each element of the quadrilateral mesh was 1 meter long, and the angles of the rhombs varied from 90 degrees to 65 degrees. The cables were a scant 5 millimeters in diameter. The entire node assembly, including clamping for the cables and the glass, was held together by a single bolt, so that the members could skew in their structural plane to accommodate the different rhombs. Only 32 different shapes of glass were used for the 524 panes, and

6.5. The interior of a grid dome in Neckarsulm has an open-sky feeling. (Photo courtesy Jörg Schlaich.)

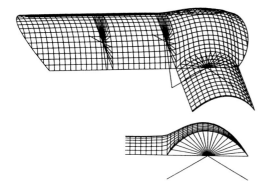

6.6. The roof of the Hamburg City Historical Museum has two intersecting vaults. (Drawing courtesy Jörg Schlaich.)

because of accurate computer programing and computer-controlled prefabrication, each pane manufactured was used—none had to be exchanged. The glass for the dome was spherically curved, with 6-millimeter single-pane safety glass on the outside and a lamination of two 6-millimeter panes of safety glass on the inside, separated by a 12-millimeter air cushion. The dome was erected and the glazing accomplished without any welding, which could have harmed the corrosion protection. The dome was erected and glazed within two months.[5]

More dramatic because of its free shape is the vault over the Hamburg City Historical Museum (plate 43). Two intersecting barrel vaults, with spans of 14 meters and 18 meters, cover an L-shaped courtyard of approximately 900 square meters (fig. 6.6). The squares of the grid, 1.17 meters to a side, are made of thin bars 60 by 40 millimeters in section. Because the twin cables, a mere 6 millimeters in diameter, disappear against the sky, and because the edge bars look like little more than the expected mullions, the glass roof seems to have no support. But the barrel vaults are singly curved and hence less strong than domes, so additional supports are necessary. Schlaich chose to bind each cylindri-

cal vault together with tension cables in the shape of a fan, maintaining the transparency of the structure (fig. 6.7). Given the effective use of lightweight cables, the covering weighs about 55 kilograms per square meter (11 pounds per square foot; 50 tons altogether, including the supporting steel frame). This is remarkably lightweight for a glass roof and supporting structure, which the historical building can easily support. Again, it is probably fair to call this structure a hybrid because the sophisticated cable-net system is separate from the vault and is reserved to address certain loads with its tensile strength, which is otherwise not engaged.

Mamoru Kawaguchi and his team at Hosei University and Maeda Corporation have done extensive studies and physical tests on the "suspen-dome" (fig. 6.8). To an even greater degree than the Schlaich domes, the suspen-dome can be characterized as two complete structural systems acting in concert for a synergetic effect. In this case, a shallow, rigid, single-layer triangulated truss is supported by a tensegrity structure—a hoop dome. In single-layer domes the bottom rings and supporting walls thrust outward, while in tensegrity domes the pull is inward. Consequently it seems logical to balance the outward thrust of the truss dome with the inward pull of the cable dome. Kawaguchi's studies show that the suspen-dome can support a load 1.5 to 1.8 times greater than a single-layer dome can without buckling.[6]

Tests were done on three brass domes 3 meters in diameter, with a rise-to-span ratio of 1:6.6. Two of the domes were fitted with a triangulated tensegrity structure and tensioned past the point where outward radial stresses in the perimeter girder were reduced to zero, prestressing the hybrid system. As downward load was incrementally induced on the three domes, the two suspen-domes sagged under a force of 50 kilonewtons (kN) and ruptured at 93.2 kN and 108.9 kN, whereas the single-layer dome sagged at 30 kN and ruptured at 60.8 kN. In the suspen-

a

6.7. (a) The glazed grid vault in Hamburg is made rigid by a diagonal cable net that all but disappears against the sky and by hubs with restraining spokes. (b) Detail of one hub with spokes. (Photos courtesy Jörg Schlaich.)

b

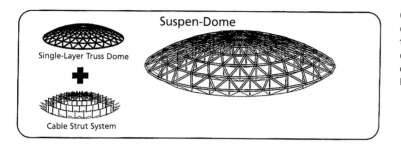

Suspen-Dome

Single-Layer Truss Dome

Cable Strut System

6.8. Mamoru Kawaguchi's suspen-dome system balances the outer thrust of a conventional truss dome with the inner pull of a cable dome. (Drawing courtesy Mamoru Kawaguchi.)

dome system the nodes most vulnerable to rupture are toward the center of the dome.

These hybrid domes have a larger load-bearing capacity as the degree of prestress is increased—it is not necessary to increase mass—so could conceivably be useful in applications where the structure needs to adapt to changing forces. Supporting walls contend with downward forces only and can be free of external buttresses. A final advantage is that the part of the dome that is the weakest can be moved by tuning the prestress, allowing for greater flexibility of design; for example, the outer regions of a dome can be made visually lightweight and open while the center is more solid. As Saitoh has said, hybrid materials are stronger and can be more precisely fabricated for a specific use than single materials; reinforced concrete, for instance, can be manufactured for a specific architectural application. Likewise, combining separate structural systems makes it possible to build not just a dome but a specific dome for each structure. Structural systems can be combined in different ways to suit different needs. Architects can ask themselves what structural capabilities or, even better, what sequence of structural capabilities would create the desired space and then find a combination of structural systems that provides that sequence.

John Chilton and his students at the University of Nottingham are investigating grillage structures and their combination with other structural systems. He defines grillages as systems of beams in which no one beam transverses the entire span but rather each beam rests on every other beam to weave a supporting roof (fig. 6.9). Typically beams spiral inward from a circle or many-sided polygon to form a smaller circle or polygon at the center of the dome. Such a structure has the advantage of requiring neither an outer tension ring nor an inner compression ring. It is impossible to load one beam alone: "in a five-beamed RF [reciprocal frame, perhaps a more accurate term], where, in plan, the beam intersections occur at a distance 2m from the supports along beams 3m long, half (5kN) of a 10kN load applied at the mid-length of one beam will be transmitted to the adjacent beam . . . [and so on around the structure] until some part of the initial load is returned to the first beam to be further distributed around the circuit."[7] An additional advantage to grillage structures is that they are visually intriguing and can be formed on many plans, with square, oval, spiral, trapezoidal, even irregular figures. Many short segments can be spiraled together or even zigzagged back and forth to a central point. The disadvantages are that the structure tends to rotate and that the failure of one beam brings down all of them.

Chilton has suggested that grillages can be retractable, functioning like the iris of the eye or a camera shutter; Piñero first envisaged such structures. Many loading positions are possible on the beams; many hole sizes are stable. It is possible to connect beams on a sliding pin mechanism that allows them to slide along one another while still transferring loads. When combined

## Tipis

John Chilton, the maker of grillage systems, with their mutually supporting, interwoven beams, points out that the traditional tipi is a hybrid grillage structure: poles rest on other poles to make arches out of straight members and maintain a hole at the top, and a membrane binds the poles together, adding to the strength of the grillage. But the tipi is not a regular cone; rather, the floor plan is egg shaped, and the structure in profile has one vertical side and one sloped side. Surely, making them this way—not just once but each and every time—is more trouble than it would be to make them regular in shape. But no doubt generations of trial and error have been institutionalized in this form. Peter Nabokov and Robert Easton note, for instance, that the vertical side always faces west to bear the brunt of the prevailing winds. A woodblock illustration, circa 1860, shows all the tipis sloping at the front and facing the same way.

Whereas putting the flat side against the wind allows for a more horizontal pole to buttress that side, there is another, more subtle aerodynamic advantage to the asymmetric design, or so I conjecture. This is suggested by the practice of staking down the tipis from inside during high winds; tipis want to fly up more than they want to blow over. Sailors know that sails are pulled as much as they are pushed; turbulence on the lee side of the sail creates low pressure, or lift (in a

horizontal direction), which sucks the sail forward. By making the tipi into a barrier against the wind the vernacular engineers of the Great Plains made, in effect, airfoils that created uplift. If my conjecture is correct, such a conversion of load from the lateral to the vertical would be highly efficient: it would allow the weight of the tipi to directly counteract the force of the wind.

If not made carefully, membrane structures can be hot in summer and cold in winter, and in some climates they can sweat as condensation drips from their surfaces. Tipis are adjustable and solve these problems in a sophisticated way. When it is hot, the lower flaps are rolled up so that cool air is constantly drawn up from the ground outside. When it is cold, an interior liner called a dew cloth is erected, and in especially cold weather the space between the two membranes is stuffed with straw. Flaps over the smoke hole can be adjusted so that the upward draft in the tipi can be maintained in light winds. Finally, tipi poles are shaved smooth so that moisture from leaks and condensation runs down them to drain at the edges of the structure rather than dripping on the sleepers below. The traditional tipi thus embodies a wealth of practical engineering knowledge, especially about the nesting of several independent structural systems, each of which is called into play when needed. Engineers might exploit the accumulated wisdom of vernacular architecture.

Village of tipis, circa 1860.

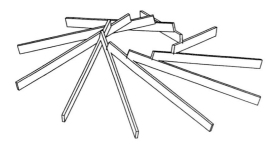

6.9. In the basic grillage system every beam is supported by all the others, and no single beam transverses the entire span. (Drawing courtesy John Chilton.)

with membranes, grillage structures could adapt to wind loads and other nonsymmetrical dynamic loads by efficiently distributing the load to all parts of the membrane.[8] Studies of hybrid structures using grillages are just beginning, but grillages seem to lend themselves to such applications (box).

At present, the conscientious designer researches the worse-case dynamic loads on a structure (wind loads, snow loads, earthquakes) for the expected life of the structure, adds in the maximum live loads foreseen (that is, with changing uses of the structure), and combines these with the dead load of the structure (its weight). The total is multiplied by a safety factor, say 2 or 3, and the loads are considered in connection with the weakest link in the structure, the material weakness of the smallest part under load. The resulting "defense in depth" is a structure grossly overbuilt for its likely use and without any guarantee of safety, for even the best engineers cannot anticipate all possible combinations of loads that focus stress on points of material weakness. And as J. E. Gordon has argued, overbuilding is not only wasteful but can be dangerous—for example, when added plating on a ship's hull focuses stress on the points of transition to the regular hull.[9] The reinforced hull can become weaker than the original.

With hybrids, however, completely separate structural systems are held in reserve and auto-matically become effective or dominant when loads warrant their use. Of course, redundancy of support is a feature in earlier building concepts; the difference with true hybrids is the movement of the building, which allows the reserve structural system to become operative or paramount. Hybrid structures, then, have a huge potential for replacing brute-strength and worst-case paradigms with safer, subtler, and more efficient models. Genuine hybrids are quite new, but interest in the idea is already intense. With hybrid structures, engineers are moving toward a paradigm for buildings to be strong in the way that adaptable living organisms are strong.

# Structural
# Morphology

A few dozen engineers and architects share the view, currently considered revolutionary, that geometry drives architecture forward.[1] To be ignorant of complex polyhedra, four-dimensional geometry, fractals, three-manifold topology, and the like—to have the cube and the octatruss the only geometric options—is to restrict structures with a severity that not even nature demands, its stern doctrine of optimization notwithstanding (box). There are also aesthetic considerations. Technobuffs may look lovingly at row after row of tetrahedra, but the public sees them as mechanical and boring, just more inhuman examples of Eiffel Tower trusswork. Why bother looking at something we just saw! But the complaint against mechanistic architecture, when considered honestly, is not that geometry is alien to human structures—geometry is unavoidable in structures; the complaint is that the geometry used is at least 100 years old and was fresh in another context entirely.

Now the computer has given fresh impetus to mathematically generated form. An example of the synergy of new mathematics and computer graphics is the decades-long project by Hoshyar Nooshin, at the University of Surrey, to develop formex algebra and its implementation in a computer program called Formian by Nooshin's collaborators, Peter Disney, of the University of Surrey, and Chiaki Yamamoto, of Taiyo Kogyo Corporation. Formex algebra is intended to generate and encode complicated patterns in two and three dimensions to assist architects and engineers in designing spaceframes. The initial elements of such a pattern might be only three nodes and two connecting lines, defined in some trivial coordinate system. By using simple functions like *Trans* (translation), *Ref* (reflection), *Rin* (rindle, or translational replication; also *Rind*), and *Lam* (lambda, or reflectional replication), complicated spaceframes can be generated. For example, $F$ = [[1,0; 0,1], [0,1; 1,2]] is read to mean that the plot of two straight lines that have those integers as coordinates will be represented by the letter $F$. The statement $H$ = $Rin(1,4,2)|F$ is read to mean that $H$ will refer to the pattern generated by the rindle (translational repetition) of the figure $F$ in the direction 1 (the $x$ direction) for 4 repeats and at intervals of 2, as in figure 7.1.[2]

Grids can be stored as formex expressions and regenerated when full data bases when needed. Multilayered grids can also be generated by this method, as can grids with open spaces in them. Once grids are defined, they can undergo cylindrical, spherical, even toroidal transformations. Grids can be fanned out using a rosette function and warped and stretched in virtually any conceivable way. Functions can be combined with unanticipated results. Thus it is possible for

Robert Le Ricolais, who died in 1977 at the age of eighty-three, studied neither architecture nor engineering but was one of the most influential professors of structures in the world. He began to study for a science degree, was interrupted by World War I, then, after the war, studied art. His interest in Russian Constructivism eventually led to his working as an engineer in Nantes and doing research in the application of industrial processes and materials to architecture. In 1951 he accepted a teaching position at the University of Illinois; later he moved to the University of Pennsylvania, where he formed a close relationship with Louis Kahn. At Penn "his research studies gave birth to some remarkable publications: repetitive configurations analyzed for the first time using topological methods; stressed structures . . . ; minimal surfaces with double curvature, which he studies using the soap bubble method; automorphism and dualism." He studied seashells, radelaria, crystals, spiderwebs, and skeletons, looking for insights into structures and working to establish a structures research independent of architecture. One of the spiritual parents of structural morphology, he is the author of the morphologists' battle cry: Infinite span, zero weight.

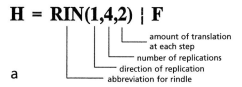

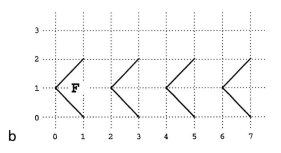

7.1. A formex expression is (a) explained and (b) illustrated. (Drawing courtesy Peter Disney.)

a program user with only a little training to invent unvisualized patterns by the manipulation of a few algebraic functions.

Because Formian was developed by engineers, as opposed to pattern generation programs written by mathematicians, structural analysis is built into the program. Grids can be loaded and axial forces and displacement read out in a variety of graphic displays or numeric tables. Constant, rapid structural feedback is available to guide searches for novel structures, making computer-generated structure searches a powerful research tool. The contrast with the earlier method of working, based on viewing, remembering, and modifying existing structures, is enormous.

Formian is in use. Takeshi Oshiro, at the University of the Ryukus, and others at Taiyo Kogyo Corporation have shown that the Isozaki-Kawaguchi design for the covering of the deployable Palau Sant Jordi (see plates 30, 31; fig. 4.10) can be described with Formian.[3] Figure 7.2 shows a general view of the roof of the stadium. The Formian expression for the center section, including the upper, lower, and diagonal members but not including the curvature of the spaceframe, is given by the following five expressions:

$A1 = ROS(1,2,1,2)|[(0,0,1; 2,0,1), (0,0,1; 1,1,0)]$
$A2 = Rind(23,13,2,2)|A1$
$B1 = ROS(1,2,1,1)|[1,1,0; 3,1,0]$
$B2 = Rind(22,12,2,2)|B1$
$AB = A2 \# B2$

To describe all five sections, specifying their intersections, and to arc the sections into their final shape, only forty such lines of code are necessary. Although it may take sixty hours of training to be comfortable with Formian to the extent that those forty lines of code are easily comprehensible, the efficiency of the system quickly offsets the initial investment of time.

Formex, the pattern algebra, is more basic than Formian, the first computer language to implement the mathematics. Frank Chu, of the Xinhong Spaceframe Company in China, has written a more sophisticated implementation of formex called SFCAD, which runs on a Sun com-

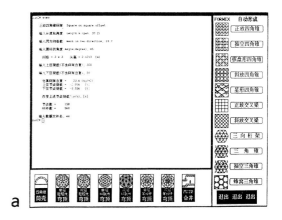

a

b

7.3. (a) Frank Chu's point-and-click formex program is easy to use, as the computer screen shows. (b) With the aid of the program Chu designed the Rongqi gym in 1992. (Drawings courtesy Frank Chu.)

puter SPARC system (fig. 7.3a). With SFCAD the engineer manipulates formex expressions using icons and buttons, much as in a Macintosh or Windows application; the engineer need not understand the algebra behind the pictures, which speeds learning to use the system and also the production of structures once the program is learned. In Xinhong's 1992 production year, over 250 spaceframe designs were created, employing over 1,500 plotter drawings, with the SPARC version of the program. Between 1990 and 1995, Chu has designed and analyzed over 600 spaceframes using various versions of the program. A beautiful example of Chu's designs is the butterfly spaceframe in Rongqi (fig. 7.3b). Unfortunately for English speakers, the interface for this program is in Chinese, but English replications would not be difficult, given the generic nature of formex.[4]

Formex is still new and so far has been used only to facilitate the planning of previously used

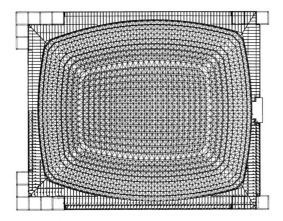

7.2. A top view of the Palau Sant Jordi spaceframe shows the intricate grid system. The entire spaceframe, composed of 12,000 parts, can be specified with only forty formex expressions. (Drawing courtesy Mamoru Kawaguchi.)

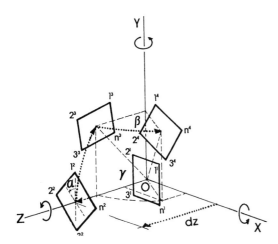

7.4. Polyhedra can be generated by rotating and translating polygons. (Drawing courtesy Pieter Huybers.)

spaceframe designs. With more widespread use, however, the temptations and opportunities for generating more original lattices will multiply, and the tool will come into its own.

Pieter Huybers, at Delft University of Technology, and his colleagues, principally Gerrit van der Ende, have developed a program called CORELLI that uses a novel approach to generate structures. They note that three-dimensional polyhedra can be formed by the rotation and displacement of two-dimensional polygons; for example, six copies of a square can be tipped up, turned around, and placed at the same distance from the origin to make a cube (fig. 7.4). This series of steps is called a rotation case, and it can be abstracted and stored in the program as a routine to be applied to shapes other than a square. The rotation cases for the four triangles of the tetrahedron, the eight triangles of the octahedron, the twelve pentagons of the dodecahedron, the twenty triangles of the icosahedron, the twelve squares of the truncated cuboctahedron, and the thirty squares of the truncated icosadodecahedron have all been obtained.[5]

Procedures can be mixed and matched to form complex polyhedra. An example is given in figure 7.5, where thirty squares are rotated

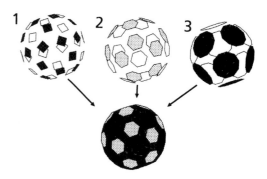

7.5. With the computer program CORELLI, designed by Pieter Huybers, sequences of rotations from different polyhedra can be combined to rotate polygons into complex polyhedra. (Drawing courtesy Pieter Huybers.)

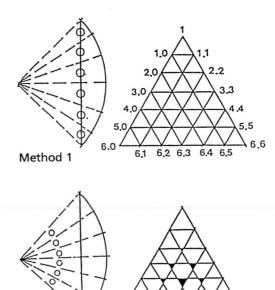

7.6. Huybers subdivides polyhedron faces in two ways here. Method 1 is to divide a face with equal line segments; method 2 is to divide a face with equal angles. (Drawing courtesy Pieter Huybers.)

according to the rotation case for the truncated icosadodecahedron, then twenty hexagons (instead of triangles) are placed in the rotation case of the icosahedron, and twelve decagons

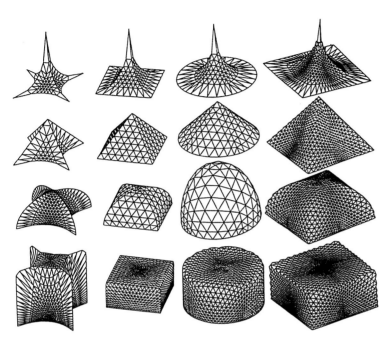

7.7. The four top shapes can be converted to the shapes below them by changing a few global parameters in the computer program. (Drawing courtesy Pieter Huybers.)

(instead of pentagons) are placed with the dodecahedron rotation case. Other rotation cases can be added to these basic ones as desired.

The faces of the polyhedron can be subdivided according to three regimes: (1) pyramidal triangular "caps" can be placed on any of the polyhedra made by CORELLI, which "pyramidizes" the polyhedron and subdivides the faces, rounding the form so that the edges approach geodesic arcs; (2) the faces of the polyhedra can be subdivided (increasing the frequency of the polyhedra) by equally dividing the edges of the faces; or (3) the face can by cut by equal spherical angles from the center of the polyhedron (fig. 7.6). CORELLI can further manipulate these complexly faceted structures by adjusting their global curvature. Such faceted structures can be considered triaxial ellipsoids, where the distance to any point on the surface is given by equations in which the exponents are 2 (numbers squared). By making the values less than or greater than 2, the faceted surfaces can be modified (fig. 7.7).

Finally, any polyhedron or collection of

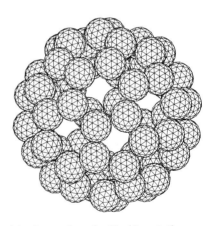

7.8. Polyhedra can be submitted to rotation cases, making complex structures. (Drawing courtesy Pieter Huybers.)

polyhedra can be treated like a polygon and submitted to a rotation case procedure. For example, sixty geodesic spheres can be rotated according to a truncated icosahedron rotation case to form the shape of the carbon-60 molecule, known as the Bucky Ball, or Buckminsterfullerine, in honor of Fuller (fig. 7.8).

## Shapes with Four Dimensions

The regular geometric figures in four-dimensional space are the six regular polytopes, each composed of only one kind of three-dimensional cell. The analogous figures in three-dimensional space are the five Platonic solids, the faces of each solid being composed of only one kind of two-dimensional polygon. The simplex—the 5-celled polytope—is the four-dimensional tetrahedron composed of five regular tetrahedral cells, three of which fit around each edge. The hypercube—the 8-celled polytope—is composed of eight cubes, three of which fit around each edge. The four-dimensional octahedron—the 16-celled polytope—is composed of sixteen regular tetrahedra, four of which fit around each edge. The four-dimensional cuboctahedron—the 24-celled polytope—has 24 regular octahedra, three of which fit around each edge. The four-dimensional dodecahedron—the 120-celled polytope—is composed of 120 regular dodecahedra, three of which fit around an edge. Finally, the four-dimensional icosahedron—the 600-celled polytope—is composed of 600 regular tetrahedra, five of which fit around each edge.

The cuboctahedron is semiregular in three dimensions and regular in four dimensions; otherwise, the matchup with the Platonic solids is consistent. It has eight triangular faces and six square faces formed by the intersection of an octahedron and a cube. As Buckminster Fuller noted, a unique property of the cuboctahedron is that the edge length is the same as the distance from each vertex to the center, suggesting a natural internal cohesion of its parts.

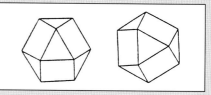

Two views of the cuboctahedron.

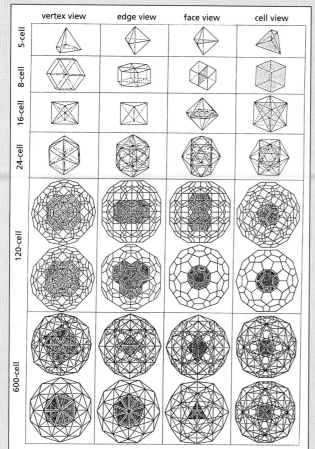

Views of the 6 four-dimensional polytopes.
(Drawings courtesy Koji Miyazaki.)

Huybers's program demonstrates the power of the computer to not only present complex geometric structures but to search for new ones and customize them for particular uses. The coordinates of the vertices in three-dimensional space are known, as are the lengths of the edges, the areas of the faces, and so on, all in metric form. This information can be passed directly into programs for structural analysis or computer-driven three-dimensional model building.

An unlikely but promising source of new geometries for structures is four-dimensional geometry—the geometry of four spatial dimensions (time is not one of them). Although students of engineering and architecture are admonished to keep their feet on the ground—on solid earth with its immutable directions of length, height, and width—mathematicians have for over a hundred years studied a space delineated by four (not three) mutually perpendicular lines intersecting at a point. Objects in this space cannot be built on earth any more than a three-dimensional cube can fully exist on a sheet of paper. A cube can nevertheless be effectively depicted on a sheet of paper, as when an open cube casts a shadow on a tabletop. When projected into three-dimensional space, four-dimensional geometric figures prove to be a rich source of fascinating new shapes (box).

Koji Miyazaki obtains fascinating three-dimensional structures from four-dimensional ones in two ways: by either packing or sectioning polytopes. He has noticed that three polytopes pack to fill four-dimensional space. That is, the hypercube and the 16-cell and 24-cell polytopes can each be juxtaposed to copies of itself such that each cell is a cell in precisely two units at once (just as cubes can be packed together so that each square is the face of two cubes simultaneously). Whether packed or not, most three-dimensional shadows of four-dimensional projections are intricately crosshatched with lines connecting vertices, but in some projections lines and faces that are distinct in four dimensions are superimposed in three, giving three-dimensional patterns that are clearer and less dense. The same effect is achieved by turning a stack of cubes to the sun so that its shadow is reduced to a pattern of squares. By selecting only some of the possible projections, useful new spaceframe patterns with startling visual appeal can be created.[6]

Miyazaki uses the more complex 120-cell and 600-cell polytopes to derive multilayered-dome configurations (fig. 7.9). These two intricate polytopes have a roughly spherical hull when projected into three dimensions; the cells closest to the hull are foreshortened the most by the projection, skewed to be quite shallow, as is fitting for a multilayered dome. Miyazaki's computer program allows him to arbitrarily slice the cells of the polytopes both before and after they are projected. In three-dimensional space, slicing a small bit off the corners of a dodecahedron yields a semiregular figure of twelve decagons and twenty triangles. In same way, slicing off corners in the higher dimension can generate a great multiplicity of complicated semiregular multilayered domes. The structural properties of these domes, whose cells are often interlaced, have not been studied, but their beauty and originality warrant exploration.

Haresh Lalvani, of Pratt Institute, has also developed a form-generating system based on the projections of figures with four or more dimensions. The four-dimensional cube, for example, becomes the static model of a complex of dynamic "growths" in which points are turned into lines, lines into rhombs, rhombs into composite complex polyhedra. In figure 7.10 the origin of the hypercube is a point marked with a dot. Extending this dot in one of any four directions turns the dot into a line. Any two combinations of lines creates a polygon, as when line 1 is drawn along line 4 to create the square (1,4) on the top right. These polygons are guaranteed to tessellate because of their derivation. That is, they will make a mosaic of congruent polygons

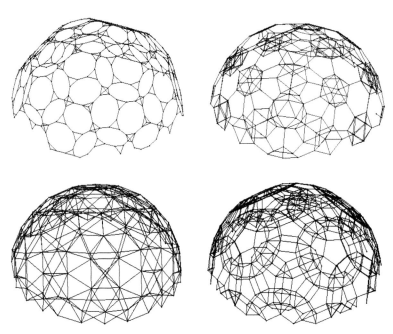

7.9. Four different projections and truncations of the same four-dimensional 120-cell polytope. (Drawings courtesy Koji Miyazaki.)

that would cover a plane, and they must make connected two-dimensional patterns because they are projections of figures that are connected in a higher dimension. By increasing the dimensions of the basic template cube from four to seven or eight, new rhombs are discovered for assembly into new two-dimensional tessellations. Again, these are not arbitrary shapes; their derivation guarantees that they will be interrelated families of rhombs and cells and hence useful.[7]

Figure 7.10 can also be read as a projection into three dimensions from four, not just a projection into two dimensions from four. We find a set of polyhedra (in this case, two skewed cubes) that can now be seen to be related to one other—a family. These assemble to make a rhombic dodecahedron composed of two each of the two different kinds of cells. The rhombic dodecahedron has now been redefined as a projected hypercube. Thus, information about novel three-dimensional tessellations can be derived directly

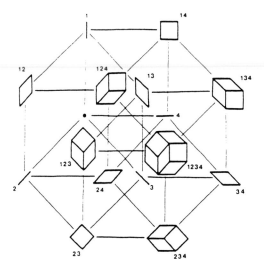

7.10. Haresh Lalvani generates polygons and polyhedra by making projections of higher-dimensional objects. (Drawings courtesy Haresh Lalvani and Neil Katz.)

# Lattices

The architect Haresh Lalvani uses hypercubic lattices as metastructures to organize polyhedra. On a cubic lattice, polyhedra can be assembled into families, and these families can be assembled on a four-dimensional grid. The transformation of one polyhedron to another, by fusion or truncation, becomes evident. By referring seemingly dissociated lower-dimensional phenomena to a higher-dimensional organizational structure, insights about their interrelation are gained.

Not just hypercubes but other hyper-polyhedra can be placed in a metastructure of higher dimensions. These lattices can be used to make tables of three-dimensional patterns. Here, four-dimensional objects, composed of three-dimensional cells, are arranged in periodic tables of five-dimensional cubic lattices. These polygons, cells, and composites of cells originate in a higher-dimensional forge using higher-dimensional templates that are regular, rectilinear, and connected (in their original dimension). As with two-dimensional unit cells, they are consequently guaranteed to be part of a three-dimensional pattern and guaranteed to fill space, which makes them applicable to making novel architectural spaceframes.

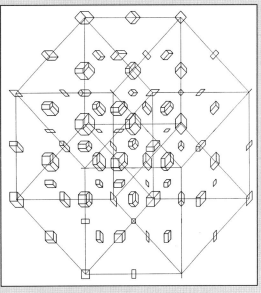

Polyhedra can be converted into other polyhedra by sliding them to different positions in Lalvani's higher-dimensional metastructures. (Drawing courtesy Haresh Lalvani and Neil Katz.)

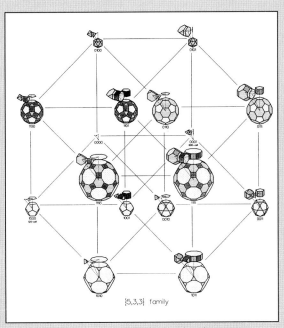

Hyper-polyhedra can, like polyhedra, be placed in a meta-structure of higher dimensions. (Drawing courtesy Haresh Lalvani and Neil Katz.)

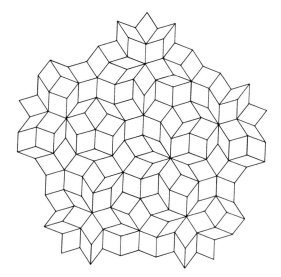

7.11. In this nonrepeating pattern with two elements, a configuration within the pattern may repeat, but not at regular intervals. (Drawing: Tony Robbin.)

from Lalvani's hypercubic projections, because the components originate in a four-dimensional figure that has three-dimensional cells (box).

At first, Lalvani's method might seem to be a needless complication of straightforward geometry. Why refer two-dimensional geometry to a higher-dimensional "metastructure" or redefine a rhombic decagon as a projected hypercube? Yet using multidimensional forms is a powerful and fruitful approach, with many compensating advantages. A disorganized zoo of shapes is in the equivalent of the periodic table of chemistry. Open locations in this periodic table are sites of new combinations, and complex tessellations of

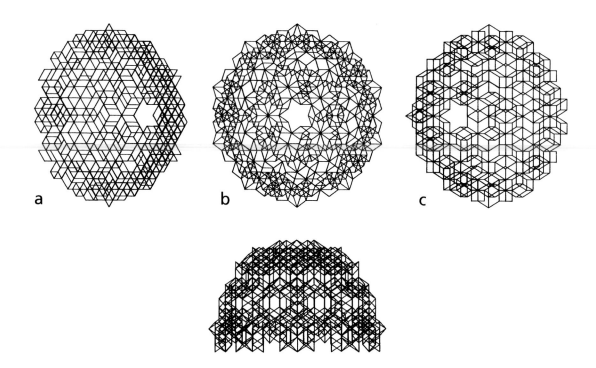

a                              b                              c

7.12. Three shadows—(a) morning, (b) noon, and (c) afternoon—cast by the quasicrystal dome, shown in elevation below the shadows. (Drawing: Tony Robbin.)

two-dimensional cells can be discovered. The projection method yields tessellations that may not be periodic (having evenly spaced repeats of basic units) but instead yield nonperiodic quasicrystal tessellations, which are the source for a marvelous new architecture, discussed below.

Lalvani's method is impressive for being low-tech. Although he has collaborated with computer programmers to automate or animate his insights, all of his work can be accomplished with the tools available to Euclid. The method is expansive and inclusive; Lalvani himself has not even begun to exhaust the possibilities. Like Newton with his secret calculus, Lalvani explains his results with more traditional arguments, knowing that a reliance on an unfamiliar mathematics might deter his audience. Yet his voluminous production suggests that four-dimensional geometry ought to be taught to first-year architecture students, before their minds are ruined by the brutal inadequacies of mere three-dimensional geometry.

Miyazaki, Lalvani, and I (who have spent twenty years making four-dimensional paintings, wall reliefs, and computer programs) have separately made the transition from four-dimensional geometry to quasicrystals, a new type of three-dimensional geometry, only fifteen years old, with astounding properties. This coincidence is explained by the nature of quasicrystals: they are really three-dimensional manifestations of higher-dimensional cubes, and their irrational properties result from being projected into three-dimensional space.[8]

There are four interesting aspects to the new quasicrystal geometry. First, the pattern is nonrepeating. Although a quasicrystal fills space with standard elements, it confounds expectations by not repeating a regular pattern. For 30,000 years, human beings all over the world have made repeating patterns to organize their experiences, but quasicrystals have patterns that are fundamentally different from all these (fig. 7.11). Second, a quasicrystal has simultaneous fivefold, threefold, and twofold symmetry, which

7.13. A quasicrystal can have a hierarchy of local configurations. (Models: Tony Robbin.)

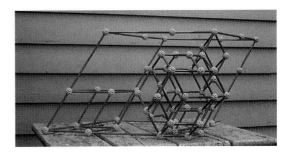

7.14. Quasicrystals can be subdivided into self-similar polyhedra that also make quasicrystals. (Model: Tony Robbin.)

means that sometimes a figure appears to be made up of right angles, sometimes triangles, and sometimes star pentagons, depending on the vantage point. Consequently, shadows from the structure magically transform as the sun changes position, as if the structure were a kaleidoscope without moving parts (fig. 7.12). Third, a quasicrystal is assembled from intermediate groupings—from the four golden zonohedra: rhombohedron, rhombic dodecahedron, rhombic icosahedron, and rhombic triacontahedron. These geometric solids float in the quasicrystal at irregular intervals (fig. 7.13). Finally, the components of a quasicrystal can always be subdivided into smaller self-similar elements, as with fractal foliation (fig. 7.14). There are two such deflations possible: one with the golden ratio, $1{:}\tau$, and the other, discovered by the Japanese physicist Tohru Ogawa, with a ratio of $1{:}\tau^3$.[9]

Under the auspices of the Center for Art, Science, and Technology at Denmark's Technical University and with the active support and collaboration of the engineer Erik Reitzel, of the Danish Royal Academy, I made studies to build a quasicrystal structure at the university (plates 44–45). At the end of the day, a long Nordic day, it was decided to build an interior sculpture with the scale and detail necessary to reveal the visual properties of quasicrystals and also to be a model for architectural quasicrystal spaceframes.[10]

The three-story atrium of the Danish Technical University is an ideal setting for such a quasicrystal sculpture. Open stairs and two bridges allow the viewer to pass under, over, around, and through the work and to happen upon the many and unexpected occurrences of fivefold, threefold, and twofold symmetry. In winter, sunlight is caught by mirrored plates and reflected down into the room and into the sculpture. A half-mirror on the bottom of the work reflects crisp, moving, colored little images, like miniature paintings, onto the walls and ceiling of the space. In summer, direct sunlight passes over the sculpture, casting direct shadows on the floor that transform the images from fivefold to threefold to twofold. On cloudy days six strong artificial lights re-create the morning, noon, and afternoon patterns.

The sculpture is in four parts, each of which demonstrates a quality of quasicrystals. First is the Dome, about half of a subdivided (two-frequency) triacontahedron. From above, the fivefold symmetry of this structure is apparent, but from below we see the near chaos inside. A large Pinwheel shape is opposite the Dome. There are fifteen ways that a rhombic dodecahedron can be oriented in a quasicrystal, and this spiral shape is composed of those fifteen rhombic dodecahedra. The Snake is a curvaceous linear section that connects the Dome and the Pinwheel. It is based on three 5-petal flower shapes, and from above it presents a perfect two-dimensional quasicrystal, a Penrose pattern.

Finally, there is the Large-Scale Section, based on Ogawa's $1{:}\tau^3$ deflation; like a fugue, the geometry breaks apart and appears to run wild, only to converge again at key nodes.

The entire structure of over 10,000 parts was designed, fabricated, assembled, and installed in an all-too-quick fifteen weeks. All the components were made in the United States by Richard Brown of RCB Precision of Mount Vernon, New York, a machinist who had made similar parts for me before, and then shipped by air freight to Denmark. With the aid of five coworkers (mainly civil engineering students), I glued the smaller components together into the four large parts. People at the Technical University made many tests of the glued joints to ensure that they were strong. These joint parts were made to fit with a gap of 0.005 of an inch. Next we fitted acrylic plates 6 millimeters thick into the sculpture. Although their main purpose is aesthetic, the plates function structurally. Pure quasicrystals are made up of rhombs and are unstable. These plates proved to be very effective in stiffening the sculpture, however; the entire 7-meter pinwheel shape could be lifted from one point without distortion.

The architectural sculpture was dedicated on January 28, 1994. It demonstrates that spaceframes, node-and-rod structures, need not be dehumanizing, monotonous repetitions of nineteenth-century ideas but can have the visual excitement of a concept of space that is truly modern—a concept of flux, rich ambiguity, and subtle order.

The practical application of any such exotic geometry to architecture creates a dilemma. Either the exotic geometry is compacted, tamed as it were, into a plane truss or some other conventional architectural element, robbing the geometry of its uniqueness, or, if given its due, the familiar rectilinear shape of rooms must be sacrificed. J. François Gabriel, professor of architecture at Syracuse University, has used the traditional nesting of octahedra and tetrahedra, the highly stable octatruss system, to generate mega structures that are not rectilinear, but rather extend the inherent indeformability of octatruss spaceframes to their logical conclusion. In his system, spaceframe trusses make the edges of an eight-story building in the shape of an octahedron lying on a side. The open space of the octahedron is filled with an open but rigid three-dimensional honeycomb truss (fig. 7.15).[11]

Gabriel notes that his system has the symmetry of the cuboctahedron, which retains the symmetry of the cube with its squares on top, bottom, and four sides, plus the symmetry of the octahedron, with eight triangle faces stacked on four diagonals, plus the symmetry of a hexagon, in that four intersecting hexagons make up its edges (that is, the cuboctahedron cut in half along is edges produces a hexagon base; fig. 7.16). In figure 7.17 the honeycomb interior truss is oriented to take advantage of the hexagonal symmetry: the rooms are hexagonal prisms stacked on the diagonal such that every room touches four others (two above and two below), and the struts lie in the walls of the rooms and are continuous diagonals through the volume of the encompassing octahedron. Other configurations are possible and have been investigated, including rooms that are cuboctahedra or half-cuboctahedra. In all cases there is a natural and self-similar progression of scale and continuity of shape from the smallest cells in the spaceframe, to rooms, to clusters of rooms for work or housing units, to villages of units.

On the use of the honeycomb structure Gabriel quotes Frank Lloyd Wright: "I am convinced that a cross-section of honeycomb has more fertility and flexibility where human movement is concerned than the square. The obtuse angle (120 degrees) is more suited to human 'to and fro' than the right angle. That flow and movement is, in this design, a characteristic lending itself admirably to life as life is to be lived in it." Gabriel himself concludes: "In architecture, it is necessary to distinguish between

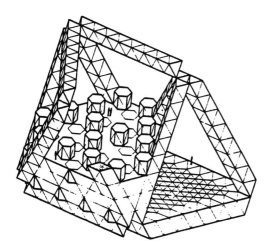

7.15. The octatruss spaceframe need not result in buildings with right angles. (Drawing courtesy François Gabriel.)

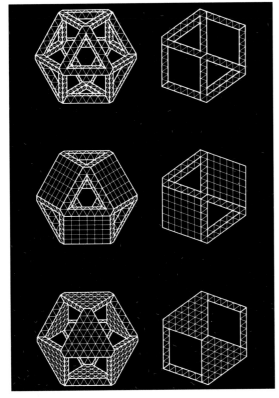

7.16. A cuboctahedron structure can be configured in many possible ways. (Drawing courtesy François Gabriel.)

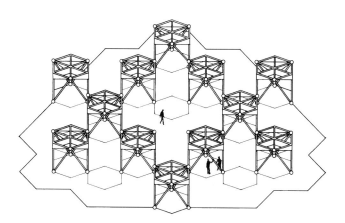

7.17. Rooms in the shape of hexagonal prisms are workable spaces and fit well into a variety of three-dimensional triangulated lattices. (Drawing courtesy François Gabriel.)

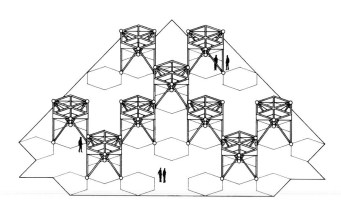

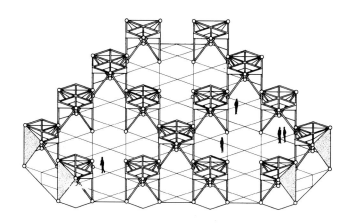

what is done for good reason and what is simply done as a result of habit." Rectilinear rooms are simply habit; abandoning them is a sacrifice without a loss. Rectilinear rooms based on beams and vertical columns are unstable, so rigid joints or other bracing are necessary; and constructing vertical interior columns above a large room on a lower floor is difficult. But, as Gabriel summarizes, such difficulties are greatly diminished with oblique columns—by replacing the unsound square matrix with a rigid triangular matrix (see fig. 7.17).[12]

Such obtuse-shaped rooms have design advantages in addition to their structural superiority, as Wright suggested. Gabriel mentions the charm of attic rooms with pitched roof and gables and the appeal of old houses with bay windows and meandering add-ons. Such nonrectilinear rooms are fun to be in. True, beds are rectangular, but desks, couches, tables, and bookcases need not also be made exclusively of right angles. Enclosing a space with a sphere is, besides, more efficient than enclosing it with the four planes of a tetrahedron, which has less volume per unit of surface area than the sphere. Cubes, with their sharp corners, are in the middle of this spectrum of efficient shapes, whereas hexagonal prisms and cuboctahedra approach the convex efficiency of the sphere. It is also true, as Gabriel notes, that membranes and tensegrity systems have so far been applied to single-story structures of one room (albeit a large, high room); by definition, tessellated polyhedra make multistoried buildings.

Another way in which structural morphology can be put to practical use has already been explored in the form of plate structures, independently discovered in the 1970s by two engineers, Janos Baracs, of the University of Montreal, and Ture Wester, of the Royal Academy of Fine Arts in Copenhagen. Plates have long been used to stiffen post and beam structures, and plates (of cast concrete, say) folded into a kind of partial box-beam have long been used for roofs and segments of elevated highways; but *plate structures*

refers to something different: the use of hinge-joined rigid plates as the primary or only structural system. In pure plate structures, nodes are not needed, and the axial forces that connect nodes are likewise absent. Javits Convention Center in New York is a notorious example of the expensive problem caused by the failure of nodes, which frequently transfer not only axial forces along the rod members but bending forces as well—tremendous forces all focused on one small point. Instead, plate structures are held up by easily managed sheer forces along the long edges of the plates. Because the angles of the hinges are irrelevant (and thus the metric properties of the structures are secondary), the mathematics of topology, which traces connectivity, is appropriate to the study of plate structures.

Wester in particular emphasizes the dualism of plate structures and lattice structures (fig. 7.18). For example, the dual of a dodecahedron is an icosahedron, because it can be formed by joining the twelve centers of its pentagonal sides to make the twelve vertices of an icosahedron, each vertex having five members. The icosahedron is stable as a lattice structure because all members form triangles; the dodecahedron is stable as a plate structure because three plates meet at every corner. The cube is stable as a plate structure; its dual is the octahedron, which is stable as a lattice structure. Note the converse: the cube is unstable as a lattice structure, and the octahedron is unstable as a plate structure. In general, the well-known rule that lattice structures are stable if three times the number of points is less than or equal to the number of connecting members, has its dual statement that plate structures are stable if three times the number of plates is less than or equal to the number of connecting edges. For a structure to be stable all the axial forces acting on a node must sum to zero; a plate is in equilibrium when the sheer forces along its edges, expressed as moments (the tendency of the plate to spin) from a point outside the plate, all sum to zero.

If, as seems true, any argument that can be

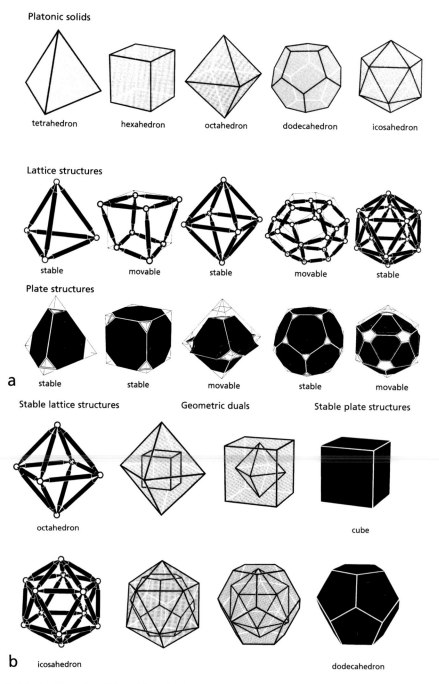

7.18. (a) The Platonic solids stable as lattice structures have triangular faces but may be unstable as plate structures; the rest are stable as plate structures. (b) In general, if a structure is stable as a lattice structure, then its dual will be stable as a plate structure. The octahedron, stable as a lattice structure, converts by dual operation into a cube, stable as a plate structure; and the icosahedron, stable as a lattice structure, converts by dual operation into a dodecahedron, stable as a plate structure. (Drawings courtesy Ture Wester.)

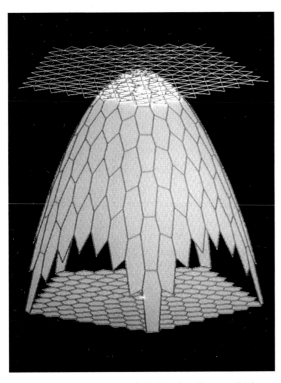

7.19. In this computer model of a glass house, thick glass plates, meeting three at a vertex, provide support. (Computer drawing courtesy Ture Wester.)

plastics, concrete, ceramics, and metal. Nor is there a limitation to the shape; any structure that can be a lattice structure can be a plate structure, including multilayered ones.

Wester points to the shell of the sea urchin as an example of a plate structure in nature (fig. 7.20). The shell is composed of calcite plates that meet three to a vertex. Microphotos of the shell show the hinged teeth on the plate edges, which allow the plates to change their dihedral angles as the plates grow and as the shell encloses a larger volume. Other studies have found that plates can be plates even when they have holes in them. No matter how lacy or slight, a structure is properly a plate structure when it is held up by the rigidity of local planar areas that are unable to rotate around their centers because of their mutual connections.

Wester's system can tell the designer of a compound structure with plates and rod members whether there are enough plates, but not where to put them. Trial and error modifications, usually on the lattice dual, are necessary. Baracs's system is an attempt to define the rigidity of any plate structure, no matter how intricate. As he notes, in 1813, Augustin Louis Cauchy first stated that a hinged polyhedron is stable if it is complete and convex. But, Baracs continues, "if we were limited to using nothing but convex polyhedra, we would find practically no application to architecture. We want to omit faces for openings, and to pack polyhedra in space, where edges may be common to three or more panels. We also want to omit articulated edges if at all possible."[14]

Baracs's system, as generalized by his mathematician collaborator Henry Crapo, is somewhat unwieldy; it depends on the analysis of structures as Schlagel diagrams—certain two-dimensional projections of the polygonal structures—and on comparing the rank or type of linkages to the number of working edges (fig. 7.21).[15] The difficult system is powerful nonetheless. Let me illustrate.

The tetrahedron is the simplest and most

made about lattice structures has a dual argument, then proposed and hard-to-study plate structures can be converted into their lattice duals for study with conventional methods and, once confirmed or modified, converted back into plate structures for construction. Wester has written a computer program that accomplishes the lattice-plate conversion automatically, proving the practicality of the method. Because there are no programs for analyzing pure plate action structures directly, Wester's program promises to greatly invigorate the study and use of plate structures.[13] He and his students can calculate, for instance, that a greenhouse of plate glass 15 millimeters thick without any metal supports would be stable under its self-weight (fig. 7.19). Fabricating efficient, cost-effective sheer connections between glass plates remains a challenge. Plates can, however, be made of any material that comes naturally in sheets, such as plywood,

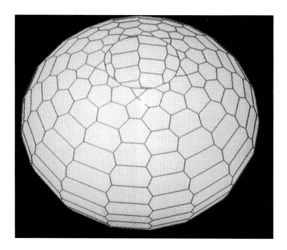

a

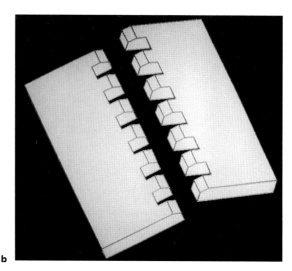

b

7.20. (a) A sea urchin shell is a pure plate structure whose plates transfer shear forces along hinges between plates. (b) A computer image of a hinge. (c) An electron microscope image of a hinge. (Computer drawings courtesy Ture Wester. Micro-image by Margit Jensen, courtesy Ture Wester.)

c

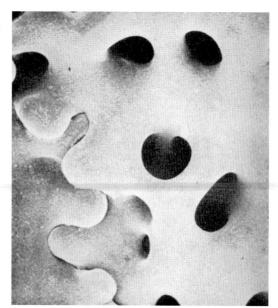

stable three-dimensional building unit. Stability equations show that three times its four points is equal to its six edges plus the minimum six supports, and because in a plate structure there would be the same number of plates as points, it would seem that all six edges are needed in the plate version. Baracs's method (much simplified) is (1) to project the tetrahedron to a plane in a Schlagel diagram (which includes one point at infinity), (2) to construct the dual diagram (which looks like the central projection of the tetrahedron), and (3) to find the Hamiltonian path (which loops around the points exactly once). Now every plate is articulated on two edges; the linkage has sufficiently high ranking in this case. The somewhat surprising result is a stable tetrahedron with four plates and only four—not six—piano hinges. A more complicated example is a three-dimensional rhombic lattice structure that is a three-dimensional projection of a regular figure in four-dimensional space. Baracs, using his system, conjectures that such a structure must be nonrigid as a pure lattice structure.[16]

The hinge assembly gives pure plate action structures tremendous potential for the architecture of deployable structures. Plate structures represent a logical and efficient use of materials and manufacturing and building systems. As Baracs points out, they are hard to design but easy to build; for buildings, it is often the other

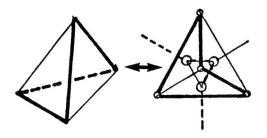

7.21. Janos Baracs's method for discovering the stability of plate structures involves tracing paths around the flattened projections of the structures and counting the traversed edges of each plate. (Baracs 1975.)

way around. Plate structures offer a great variety of architectural possibilities and are suited to the new geometries that the culture is coming to require be made manifest in spaces of experience. It is to be hoped that soon engineers and architects alike will feel more confident about employing this powerful new idea (fig. 7.22).

For Wester, Gabriel, Lalvani, and all the others who are studying morphology, the goal is to enrich architecture and engineering with modern geometries. It is, indeed, the duty of people who build structures to reestablish the wholesome connection between culture and the spaces that we inhabit. Brand-new Jefferson-style law school buildings are absurd, atavistic. In all professions other than architecture, it seems, embracing the level of knowledge and the current values of society is prerequisite for effective practice. Architecture cannot be society's reservoir for nostalgia. Buildings need instead to embody the intricate, multiply connected, fluid, and subtly ordered spaces that we know and feel to be here.

7.22. Baracs collaborated with the sculptor P. Granche on an open plate structure for a subway station in Montreal in 1982. (Photo courtesy Janos Baracs.)

# Materials

Today's engineers, who already have Kevlar cords stronger than steel, will soon use concrete springs to absorb crashes, erect glass walls stronger than solid aluminum, and work with nickel-titanium sheets that can fold and unfold themselves on command and with rigid protective coverings that can heal themselves when fractured. Science-fiction materials are becoming reality, and just in time: forests are dwindling, and the true costs (cleaning up environmental damage) of coal, crude steel, and gypsum price traditional materials higher and higher. The new model of efficient structures will incorporate materials that erect, mechanically service, maintain, and repair themselves.

## Fabrics and Foils

In the United States the most widely used architectural fabric is fiberglass coated with Teflon (generically called PTFE, polytetrafluoroethylene), developed in 1973 for the University of La Verne by David Geiger (box) under the direction and auspices of Harold Gores and his Educational Facilities Laboratory at the Ford Foundation. Gores brought together Du Pont, the maker of Teflon; Owens-Corning Fiberglass; J. P. Stevens, the fabric weaver; and Chemical Fabrics Corporation (now called Chemfab), a coater already applying Teflon to fabric surfaces for assembly-line cookie baking. This remarkable

collaboration brought forth a new material application in little over a year, and the La Verne membrane turned out to be more than a prototype; as we have seen, it has been used widely in membrane structures and is retaining more of its strength than was originally estimated.

Teflon protects the extremely strong glass fibers from water, their dangerous enemy. The product is chemically inert, so most pollutants and all soot and dirt wash off without damaging the coating. The material is resistant to abrasion, but could be more so. The coated material can be engineered to transmit as much as 18 percent of the light striking it and is highly reflective, absorbing little light as heat. Especially appealing is the ability of Teflon-coated fiberglass to be heat-welded on site (making flaps over mechanically joined seams); multiple-panel membranes can be fused into one permanently sealed watertight skin. Heat welding saves expensive labor and complicated clamping systems and reduces the installed cost of Teflon-coated fiberglass to a competitive level, even though the roll cost of the uncut material can be high (about $5.50 per square foot). The coating can be applied in widths of 3.8 meters, reducing the number of panels and seams. Chemfab still manufactures the coated fabric from Du Pont's Teflon and Owens-Corning Fiberglass's product, and Birdair Corporation manufactures and installs architectural membranes of this fabric. Birdair domi-

**David Geiger**

The engineer David Geiger, like his former partner, Horst Berger, was an idealist; the son of a preacher, he volunteered time and skill to Habitat for Humanity, an organization devoted to providing low-cost housing to the needy, and considered it a mission to build ecologically efficient structures. Geiger pioneered insulated membrane domes: two or even four layers of membranes separated by layers of air or by translucent insulating material. These domes were designed to reflect sunlight in summer and absorb sunlight in winter, capturing heat in air pockets to heat or dehumidify the interior air (see fig. 8.1). Geiger also championed the design of membrane materials with desired acoustical properties. He solved both materials problems and structure problems, not prejudging a design solution or becoming identified with any one artistic style, but choosing the best structure for each site and use.

nates the field: it has built all the American projects described in this book and has expanded its activity to east Asia and Europe.[1]

PTFE-coated fiberglass has two disadvantages in addition to its high initial cost. Because the membrane material is somewhat brittle, to maintain its integrity considerable care and experience is necessary in the packing, shipment, and installation of panels. The membrane must also be accurately patterned, for fiberglass has little elastic forgiveness. Each roll has slightly different properties so must be tested separately. These variables must then be programmed into the cutting patterns for that roll.

Silicone-coated fiberglass, which dates from 1981, has been used for Callaway Gardens in Georgia (Craig, Gaulden, and Davis, architects; Horst Berger, engineer) and Geiger's tensegrity domes for the Seoul Olympics (see fig. 3.10). Silicone rubber is more flexible than Teflon, and fiberglass coated with it is less likely to be damaged during shipment and erection than fiberglass coated with Teflon. The greatest advantage, however, is that the fabric can be made very translucent, with some proponents claiming as much as 25 percent translucency for the architectural membrane and 90 percent for the thin liner material. With multiple layers of translucent membrane and glass fiber there can be both daylight illumination and very high heat retention (R values).[2]

DCI, a membrane fabricator and contractor, has the patent on silicone-coated fiberglass membranes. (DCI also works with PTFE-coated fiberglass manufactured for it by Verseidag Industries.) According to the company, recent advances have partly or wholly resolved early concerns about building with silicone-coated fiberglass. Seams can now be chemically bonded (heat accelerated) to be stronger than the material itself, as with Teflon-coated fiberglass. Some engineers still question whether this process can be adequately applied with patch kits, used on site. DCI also claims to have improved silicone's self-cleaning properties to be equal to Teflon's, yet it still recommends a once-a-year cleaning. Competitive claims and counterclaims may obscure the fact that whatever the coating, fiberglass gives both fabrics their Class A fire ratings; burning silicone, however, produces more benign fumes than burning Teflon. (In England, Teflon use was at first restricted for this reason.) DCI insists that silicone-coated fiberglass is 20 percent cheaper than PTFE-coated fiberglass, in large part because the coating processes are done at a much lower temperature. But cost comparisons on finished roofs are notoriously complicated; Birdair thinks that 25 percent reductions in its prices will occur within a year or two owing to increased efficiency in the design of standard cable connectors and other such components.

Polyester fabrics coated with polyvinyl chloride melt in the presence of flame; therefore, in the United States they are generally used for temporary structures. In Europe, however, they are used for permanent ones. Polyvinyl chloride coating can be as translucent as either Teflon or silicone coating, but it needs further coating protection to be dirt resistant. Polyester can creep (stretch over time), which can necessitate more poststressing maintenance than other membrane materials require, although the extra give can be an advantage in patterning and erection. The elasticity of the material ensures that it is not easily damaged by rough handling. Like PTFE-coated fiberglass, PVC-coated polyester is best seamed with heat, but at a lower temperature than is used for other membrane fabrics. In fact, around 70 degrees centigrade (158 degrees Fahrenheit) the seams begin to soften and have "virtually no remaining strength" under sustained loads, so the material may not be suited for all climates.[3] Currently, too, it comes in narrower widths than PTFE-coated fiberglass, between 2 and 3 meters, and so requires more seams.

Although various top coats can be applied to PVC-coated polyester, they add to the cost of the material. Acrylic top coats are both the least expensive and the least effective, but the relatively new polyvinylidene fluoride (PVDF) top coats are reported to be better. Both become yellow and tacky with age because of dirt retention, but weathering tests suggest that PVDF will extend the membrane life to fifteen years, compared with the five-year standard life expectancy of PVC-coated polyester that is either untreated or top-coated with acrylic. Tedlar is Du Pont's trade name for polyvinyl fluoride (PVF), a stiff, transparent film that can be laminated to one side (only) of the PVC-coated polyester. It improves weathering performance (DCI gives fifteen years as the life span) but makes fabrication even less convenient, because the coating cannot be heat-welded.

PVC-coated polyester has two main advantages: it can be fabricated in a great variety of colors, and it is much cheaper on the roll than other membrane materials. FTL Architects uses PVC-coated polyester for its temporary fashion show pavilions in New York's Bryant Park. And as Philippe Samyn has demonstrated in his Venafro project (see plate 17), for permanent smaller projects PVC-coated polyester can be the material of choice. Another engineer, David Campbell, feels that PVC-coated polyester is underrated and underutilized in North America.[4]

Membranes are most effective in combinations. Both silicone-coated and Teflon-coated fiberglass are commercially available with translucent fiber insulation; air is sometimes used between membranes for insulation. The membrane sandwich frequently includes vapor barriers and acoustical liners as well. (Acoustics-damping membranes have small holes in them; sound loses energy when passing through the holes, as in a minnow trap: sound waves go in and cannot find their way out.) In 1977, Geiger began investigating the use of three-layer membranes as solar collectors (fig. 8.1). The upper and middle membranes are both split: the south-

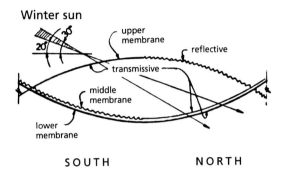

Winter sun

SOUTH          NORTH

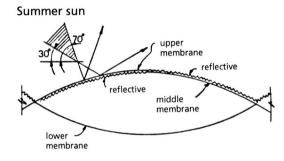

Summer sun

8.1. David Geiger proposed using three-membrane air pillows as solar heating cells. They would collect solar energy in the winter and reflect it in the summer. (Drawing courtesy Geiger Engineers.)

obtained. The silica gel is dried by additional hot air from the solar cells, which is pumped through the gel and evacuated outside.[5] Unfortunately, such opportunities to use membrane cells as heating and cooling machines have been neither fully tested nor implemented.

The newest membrane material is not a woven fabric but a foil—a polymer film sheet, usually formed into inflated cushions. Although investigated and used since the 1950s, foils have become truly useful for the first time with the introduction of an ETFE foil, made of a copolymer of linked monomer units of ethylene and tetrafluoroethylene. Craig Schwitter, of Buro Happold Consulting Engineers, Bath, has studied and used ETFE foils and catalogued their attributes:

1. Unlike other foils, ETFE foils are impervious to ultraviolet light. "Less than a 10% decrease in material strengths has been observed after 10,000 hours of [accelerated] artificial weathering. Natural exposure samples (located in Arizona and Bombay) have performed well and material is expected to have a life-span of 25 to 50 years."

2. ETFE foils are also impervious to water and most destructive chemical pollutants in the air.

3. They have a high resistance to tear; that is, they yield at approximately 3 percent strain and "have a large elongation to ultimate failure [at 28 newtons per square millimeter]," meaning that small holes do not propagate. Vector, the German manufacturer, says that as a general rule, foil balloons can support 75 kilograms per square meter, and it demonstrates with panels supporting twelve fully suited American-football players.[6]

4. ETFE foils can be manufactured in a variety of transparencies (20–95 percent transmission). Pigment can be applied to the material during manufacture, or dot patterns can be printed on the foil after it is made.

5. Finally, ETFE foils have passed fire code

facing half of the upper membrane is transmissive, the north-facing half reflective, and the south-facing half of the middle membrane is reflective, the north-facing half transmissive. During the summer the solar cell is closed and the air layer between membranes is inflated so that the middle membrane rests against the upper membrane, making a continuous reflective surface that reduces heat load. During the winter the cell is open; the middle membrane rests against the lower membrane, and solar energy absorbed by the cell can be radiated or conducted to the space below. For the Florida Junior College at Jacksonville, similar solar cells were proposed to dehumidify interior air. Air warmed by the cells is passed through silica gel, where it loses enough moisture that, when mixed with intake air, the desired moisture level is tests in both the United Kingdom and Germany; the material is flame resistant, and when it melts, it does not form hot droplets, which could fall on those below.[7]

The president of Birdair, L. James Newman, Jr., is also enthusiastic about ETFE foils. He points to their low cost, their translucency, and their color, which makes interesting architectural applications possible. Birdair is researching their use in the United States.

All foil cushions are thermal insulators, especially when formed into double cushions with three layers of foil. The seams, heat-welded to make them airtight, are clamped into frames made of aluminum extrusions. Buro Happold Consulting Engineers has developed two types of frame supports: a rigid frame like a replacement window and a cable-strengthened flexible frame that allows the cushions to move under wind load and thermal expansion—in effect, a faceted tension membrane. In areas where snow loads are heavy, thin stainless-steel wires can support the foil panels, which are limited in width to 3.6 meters but can be more than 15 meters in length. ETFE foils lose strength at 60 degrees centigrade (140 degrees Fahrenheit), hence would probably not be useful in extremely hot climates.

In 1992, Buro Happold used a rigid frame and foil system for the Westminster Chelsea Hospital atrium roof, with an overall nave and crossing transepts—the plan size was 116 by 85 meters—and with short spans of approximately 20 meters (fig. 8.2). Continuous air pressure was supplied to the air cushions through the aluminum frames. The largest cushion, 3 by 4 meters, was inflated to a depth of 600 millimeters at a low pressure of 400 pascals (about 5 pounds per square foot). Currently being designed is a flexible covering 6,000 square meters in size for ten indoor tennis courts with panels 3 by 18 meters. The cable net is hung from poles and anchored into the ground. The clamping extrusions have been designed for the full range of movement anticipated. Schwitter

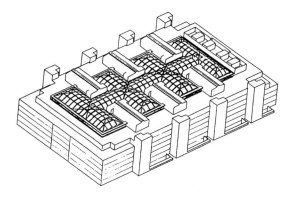

8.2. The Westminster Chelsea Hospital roof is made from ETFE foil in the form of air cushions. (Drawing courtesy Craig Schwitter and Vector GmbH.)

excitedly promotes foils as the "next thing," and when completed, the Eastleigh Tennis Halls may lend credibility to that claim.

## Concretes

At first glance, nothing could be more low-tech than cement, which has been in continual use since it was discovered by the Romans. New cement mixtures, however, are as flexible as plastic and are four times as strong in compression as the concretes used only twenty years ago. Francis Young, professor of materials science at the University of Illinois, has a business card made of cement that flexes like a credit card. Given these impressive technological advances and the depletion of other natural resources, it is imperative to push ahead with concrete. As J. D. Birchall and Anthony Kelly, of the University of Surrey, point out, it takes six times the energy to make a cubic meter of polystyrene as to make a cubic meter of concrete, and for stainless steel the energy ratio is 29:1.[8] The raw material for 97 percent of all plastic and synthetic rubber is relatively scarce petroleum. We need to develop new inorganic materials: cements and concretes that can behave like metal or plastic.

Birchall and Kelly argue that the abalone

shell, which is made at low temperatures, is 99 percent calcium carbonate, "yet its tensile strength is more than 100 megapascals (14,500 pounds per square inch) and its toughness is more than 1,000 joules per square meter of new surface generated by fracturing, which makes it comparable in that respect to polystyrene and Plexiglas."[9] Comparisons of abalone shell and cement under a microscope show that the shell has small flat plates uniform in size packed together, whereas concrete has large pores (as much as 30 percent of the volume) and irregularly shaped clumps of material. By reducing the size of the pores (grading the cement grains by size and kneading out the larger pores), cements can be made with a bending strength comparable to that of aluminum. Indeed, Birchall and Kelly have made a six-coil spring of cement that stretched but did not crack as it was pulled slightly open with 300 pounds of tension. They call this new material micro-defect-free (MDF) cement and see it as a replacement for ceramics at low temperatures. But cast concrete with the tensile strength of aluminum would also change architecture.

A second strategy to improve concrete is to use fiber reinforcement instead of steel-rod reinforcement. The new fiber-reinforced concrete composites are often stronger, lighter in weight, and more ductile and, best of all, can be applied by spraying. Thin and irregular shapes are difficult and time consuming to fill with steel rod and wire manually, and the process is becoming increasingly expensive in even the most straightforward applications. Nor do synthetic fibers rust, as reinforced steel bars do. Eventually such fibers will even perform a variety of sensing and self-adjusting tasks. Carolyn Dry, professor of architecture at the University of Illinois's Architectural Materials Laboratory, has, for example, studied the possibility of making concrete with hollow glass or polymer fibers filled with liquid adhesive. When the concrete cracks, the fiber vials rupture, releasing the adhesive and sealing the crack.[10]

William Panarese of the Portland Cement Association has summarized the different types of fibers studied and used. He notes that cement mixes already in use can contain high-tensile and stainless steel fibers as 0.5–2.0 percent of the volume. "The addition of 1.5% by volume can boost a composite's direct tensile strength about 40%. Increases up to 150% have been noted on first-crack flexural-strength measurements."[11] A dry mix process in which a fiber and dry concrete mixture is combined with water in the spraying nozzle allows as much as 2 percent steel fiber to be used in shotcrete and reduces fiber dispersion problems.

Polypropylene fibers are the most popular of the synthetic fibers, he says, because they are the cheapest and can be made in continuous filaments and mesh, which have both a higher load-carrying capacity after cracking and higher ductility than short fibers. But to reduce the cracking caused by shrinkage during drying and to improve strength, the volume should be greater than 2 percent. At lower volumes, as research has confirmed, adding fiber has little affect on the performance of the concrete.[12] Thinner polyester fibers have roughly three times the modulus of elasticity and twice the tensile strength of polypropylene; they, too, function best when more is added per unit of volume. Nylon, however, a synthetic fiber newly available for concrete reinforcement, is effective in low proportions, such as 1 pound per cubic yard, because the fiber count is so high: 1 pound of Caprolan-RC (made from nylon-6) contains more than 30 million fibers.

Panarese categorizes polyethylene, aramid (Kevlar), carbon, and acrylic fibers as specialty synthetic fibers, for none was commercially available in May 1992. Aramid fibers are by far the strongest and, as 2 percent of concrete by volume, increase strength and modulus, as tests of samples attest. Carbon fibers have been shown to double the flexural strength of laboratory samples of concrete. Both aramid and carbon fibers are more expensive than commoner fibers. Acrylic fibers are not very strong in tension, but tests have shown acrylic-reinforced concrete to be useful as a replacement for an asbestos-cement composite. Thick polyethylene fibers can be fabricated with "wartlike deformations" along the axis, which improve the fiber-concrete mechanical bond. Another possible fiber material is glass. The fibers are strong and resilient, but questions remain about their long-term strength.

Another long-used construction material, employed much longer than either glass or concrete, is also being considered as a concrete reinforcement: bamboo. Kosrow Ghavami, of the Pontifical Catholic University in Rio de Janeiro, has revived the study of its possible use. Bamboo is a renewable resource; some varieties grow as much as 4 feet a day and reach maximum strength in three years. In comparisons of tensile strength as a function of weight, it has been found that bamboo is 50 percent stronger than aluminum, which is itself stronger than mild steel, yet bamboo is produced with one-fiftieth the energy required to make steel. When used in concrete, bamboo absorbs water from the fresh concrete and expands, then shrinks again as the concrete cures, leaving gaps; results are greatly improved when the bamboo is treated with a water repellent. Ghavami estimated that bamboo-reinforced concrete beams would be twice as strong as beams without bamboo, then found in tests that they are four times as strong, though not as strong as beams with steel reinforcement. Ghavami speculates that the gain is due to the natural cusps in bamboos slats, which interlock reinforcement and concrete. Bamboo reinforcement slats lying horizontally and constituting 3 percent of the volume of the concrete have proved to be the strongest arrangement. Ghavami thinks that treated and impregnated bamboo can last ten years and notes that steel is also subject to natural degradation. Longevity must nevertheless remain a concern with all biodegradable fiber reinforcements.[13]

Slurries in which fiber content reaches 20 percent have also been studied, and in strength and ductility they greatly exceed conventional concretes. Surendra F. Shah, professor of civil engineering at Northwestern University, has tested a slurry with 10–15 percent fiber that has a thousand times the ductility and five times the tensile strength of conventional concrete. The new material can be used to make pylons that would bend instead of break during earthquakes.[14]

High-strength post-tensioned concrete can be used in dramatic spans, which opens up exciting architectural possibilities. Consider the Grande Arch in Paris, designed by J. O. Spreckelsen, architect, and Erik Reitzel, structural engineer (fig. 8.3). The Open Cube, or La Défense, as is is also called, is a massive 110 by 110 by 110 meters, made delicate by the vast open space (75-meter span) at the center, an open space that reinforces the line-of-sight axis from the Palais du Louvre to the Concorde and the Arc de Triomphe to the modern Place de la Défense. The structure looks all the more remarkable once we know that an underground highway and three railway tunnels run beneath it. The building is an integral structure floating on twenty-eight vibration-damping rubber bearings supported by twelve piers 35 meters deep. Yet the construction depth of the top and bottom sections is only 8.5 meters. This impressive feat of engineering is accomplished by a combination of shape and materials.

The building has no posts and beams in the ordinary sense; instead, megastructures on 21-meter modules bind the cube into an integrated whole (fig. 8.4a). The megas are cast with vertical and horizontal openings for doorways and mechanical systems, respectively (fig. 8.4b). The rows of slip-formed vertical megas are held laterally by end megas set at an angle of 45 degrees. Imagine a wire-frame cube dipped into soapy water. Its six faces are spanned by a bubble film. When the cube is dipped again, a bubble cube is

8.3. For the Grande Arch in Paris, high-strength concrete was used in continually cast megastructures to achieve a dramatic span. Erik Reitzel, engineer; J. O. Spreckelsen, architect. (Photo courtesy Erik Reitzel.)

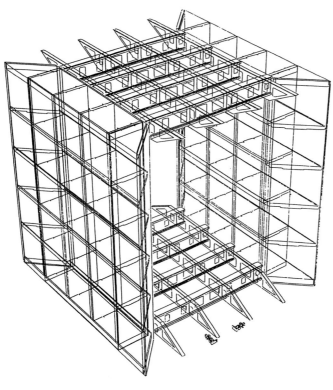

8.4. (a) Instead of posts and beams to hold the structure together, the Grande Arch has megastructures, and four of these on the faces of the open cube are at angles to the others. (b) Openings in the megas provide doorways. (Drawings courtesy Erik Reitzel.)

a

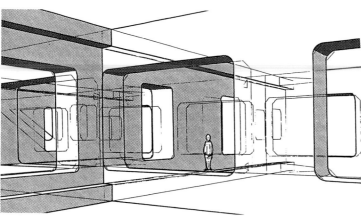

b

formed within it; the inner cube is supported by eight connecting bubble-membrane "plates" with dihedral angles at 45 degrees to the sides of the wire-frame cube. It is precisely this minimal surface configuration that is formed by the end megas. High-strength concrete with a compres-

sion strength of 50 megapascals (7,246 pounds per square inch) was used throughout, which made it possible to cast the megas with larger openings than could have been achieved with conventional concrete. Using larger openings eased architectural design problems and also lightened the overall weight of the structure.[15] We can look forward to improved concretes, and imagination and courage in their structural use will make them part of the best future architectural designs.

## Glass

Glass is rarely used structurally, even though it is relatively strong. If we compare the modulus of elasticity, measured in newtons per square millimeter, for glass, steel, and aluminum, we can see the somewhat surprising results: glass, 73,000–75,000 N/mm²; aluminum, 67,000–73,000 N/mm²; and steel, 210,000 N/mm². Now compare tensile strength: ordinary glass, 40 N/mm²; fully tempered glass, 200 N/mm²; aluminum, 215 N/mm²; and some mild steels, 360 N/mm².[16] Glass is a frozen liquid, and during manufacture, it cools before it crystallizes. Over time it tends to complete its crystallization, a process known as devitrification, which shrinks and weakens the glass. Tempered glass is glass that is reheated after manufacture and then rapidly cooled so that the surfaces shrink and bind the hot inner core. The forces induced inhibit devitrification as they strengthen the glass. Unfortunately, tempered glass is even more vulnerable to failure due to surface imperfections than ordinary glass.[17] Jörg Schlaich, working with the architect Helmut Jahn, has accomplished a startling structure, the Kempinski Hotel in Munich, which has glass end walls 30 by 35 meters, the glass panels of which are supported by vertical and horizontal prestressed cables (plate 46). (Peter Rice pioneered the use of cable-stayed glass walls in his Museum of Science and Technology in Paris, Ove Arup and Partners, engineers.)

One of the most impressive cable-stayed glass walls is the south end wall of the Denver Airport: 65 by 220 feet. This curved glass wall has to be freestanding because the roof is a membrane, offering no support. Another curved glass wall has been completed for the Channel Four Building in London (plate 47). Two of the most

8.5. Glass is a structural element in this flat roof in Hulst. Mick Eekhout, engineer and fabricator; Walter Lockleer, architect. (Drawing courtesy Mick Eekhout.)

elegant creations, however, are much smaller projects by the Dutch engineer and fabricator Mick Eekhout and his company, Octatube.

Designed by Eekhout and the architect Pieter Zaanen in 1989, the Glass Music Hall in Amsterdam is a glass box with a flat roof (plate 48). Because buckling, which breaks glass, is induced by compression, the 1.8-meter-square glass panels are hung one from the other. The top panel, the fifth, supports the deadweight of the four below; the panel beneath it supports the weight of the three below, and so on. The panels, which are fully tempered glass 8 millimeters thick, are stabilized by cable guys 8 millimeters in diameter compressing short 10-millimeter-thick perpendicular studs. "Quattro" (four-part) nodes at the ends of the studs tie four corners of four rectangular glass panels together; no mullions are used between glass plates. The 9-meter-high hall is housed inside Amsterdam's old Options Exchange, built in 1903, and it is used as a rehearsal space and for small concerts by the Dutch Philharmonic. The glass curtain walls (really hanging like a curtain) and the flat glass roof are supported by thin steel columns; unfortunately, nervous building inspectors forced the designers to place a flat roof truss on top of the columns to support the roof.

The next year, however, Eekhout, working with the architect Walter Lockleer, was permitted to make a flat, thin quattro roof for the Flower Gate pavilion in Hulst, Holland (fig. 8.5).

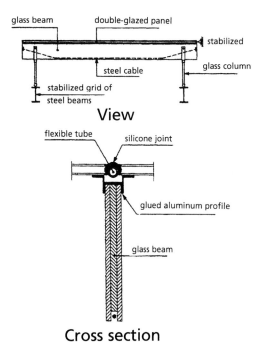

glass beam  double-glazed panel

stabilized

steel cable

glass column

stabilized grid of
steel beams

### View

flexible tube

silicone joint

glued aluminum profile

glass beam

### Cross section

a

The roof, which measures 15 by 6 meters and is 5 meters high, is supported from below by cables and short struts at the junction of four panels. The roof is double glazed: panels are 1.4 by 1.4 meters with an upper pane of light reflective glass 8 millimeters thick, a sealed air-filled cavity 12 millimeters thick, and a laminated clear glass lower panel. The roof has a 1 percent slope and a surrounding gutter. The delicate mullions would buckle if they alone formed the top cords of a truss; the glass is an important structural component.

Erick van Egeraat, of the Dutch firm Mecanoo, and Robert Nijsse, of ABT Consulting Engineers in Holland, have developed glass

8.6. (a) Glass can be used for columns and beams, a design element developed by Robert Nijsse of ABT Consulting Engineers. (b) Glass columns and beams were used for an office in Budapest. Robert Nijsse, engineer; Erick van Egeraat, Mecanoo, architect. (Drawing and photo courtesy Robert Nijsse.)

b

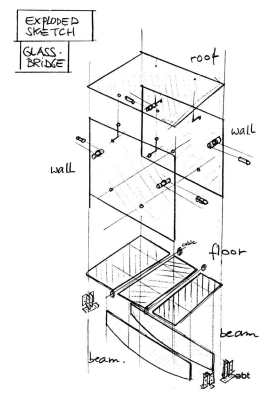

8.7. A small footbridge between office buildings has been built completely out of glass. Robert Nijsse, ABT Consulting Engineers, engineer; Dirk Jan Postel, Kraayvanger Urbis Archtects, architect. (Drawing courtesy Robert Nijsse.)

columns and cable-stayed glass beams for a glass "egg" of meeting rooms at the top of a converted mansion in Budapest (fig. 8.6). The glass columns are made of solid glass rods inserted in glass tubes; the two courses of glass are bonded together with clear epoxy glue. Aluminum fittings are glued to the ends of columns to make connections to roof and floor. Double-glazed ceiling roof panels are supported on these columns and are butted against a flexible tube sealed with silicone so that small movements do not stress the glass. The glass beams are vertical plates compressed by steel cables. Nijsse has constructed glass trusses using glass rods as the vertical compression elements and polyaramid fiber

cables as the tension elements. He and Dirk Jan Postel of Kraayvanger Urbis Archtects have built a small footbridge in Holland out of glass—beams, floor, walls, roof (fig. 8.7). The only metal is in the brackets and two cables. Although ABT has struggled with building inspectors and insurance companies (yet their Budapest client was a Dutch insurance company), they have managed to convince responsible parties that these glass structures are not only strong but safe—that the glass will give adequate, visible early warning of possible collapse, as do more conventional structural materials.

Ironically, even though glass is used to keep rain out, it is strongest if rain is kept off it. Terry Michalske and Bruce Bunker working at Sandia National Laboratories have shown that in the absence of water the strength of glass improves by a factor of 350: "Under high-vacuum conditions flaw-free glass can withstand tensile loads greater than two million pounds per square inch ($13800 \, \text{N/mm}^2$), which is 10 times the strength of most commercial metal alloys. . . . Water can accelerate the rate of crack growth more than a million times by attacking the structure of the glass at the very root of the crack."[18]

Glass fails by the enlarging of small initial surface cracks (pristine fibers of glass can be 1,000 times stronger than ordinary scratched glass for this reason), and cracks in glass can propagate as fast as half the speed of sound in glass or as slow as one-trillionth of an inch, the size of one atomic bond, per hour. The difference in the speed of propagation is the presence of water, which can be in the form of the water vapor normally found in air, or other small molecules, like ammonia. In fact, researchers have shown that stressed glass held underwater for a mere two weeks is reduced threefold in strength; continued submersion reduces strength further—it actually approaches zero.[19] It would seem that with further advances in coating technology, pristine glass could be coated to prevent water and other small molecules from entering cracks and that glass could be transparent and very strong, yet not brittle. Michalske and Bunker have done laboratory experiments proving that the growth rates of cracks can be slowed by a factor of 1,000 by applying a molecular coating to the crack. One can imagine buildings with indoor I-beams of coated glass—generally, a complete repositioning of glass in the architect's lexicon, from nonstructural cladding material to interior structural material.

## Shape Memory Alloys

Since the early 1960s it has been possible to create metals that "remember" a previous shape and return to that shape at a specified temperature. In general, alloys of copper-zinc-aluminum, copper-aluminum-nickel, or nickel-titanium are heated, then rapidly quenched, to induce a specific crystalline structure called a martensitic structure. After being deformed, the metal will return to its martensite state and shape when reheated to that trigger temperature; if its movement meets resistance, it will exert a force. Adjusting alloy ingredients, repeating the cycles of heating and cooling, and applying stress at different times in the process are all used to train the metal.[20] Recently, shape memory alloys have been improved: triggers can be two-way (the material flips back and forth at different temperatures), the triggers are relatively small temperature variations, the trigger temperature can be "anywhere below 200 degrees C.," and the alloys are available in commercial quantities and at commercial prices.[21]

Shape memory alloys have been called a solution in search of a problem. They can be adjusted in manufacture for superelasticity, for high damping properties (to be used in vibration control), or for shock resistance (needed for bulletproof cladding). For many years they have been used as fasteners and couplings, especially where small size and high performance are desired and where there is no room to fasten

parts by conventional means, as in the aeronautics industry. Researchers think that their most important attribute, however, is their ability to deliver power. The full potential for this use have not yet been imagined. Actuators for shape memory alloys are reliable; they cannot fail to perform even after decades of being kept dormant and uninspected. In power-weight ratios they are stronger than direct-current motors (they are not exactly motors themselves); they deliver power smoothly, without jerks; and they are noiseless.

Scaled up for architectural applications, shape memory alloys could be used for post-tensioning concrete, or so Wilfried Van Moorleghem, of Advanced Materials and Technologies Company in Belgium, suggests.[22] Three years after a building has been constructed—say, when the concrete slabs and arches have begun to sag—an electric current could be applied to the reinforced steel bars to re-tension the sagging concrete. I can imagine elegant construction details: bolts without nuts, completely flush "welds" of different metals. Perhaps the vibration control capabilities of these alloys will lead to new strategies for tall or long-span metal structures. Still, it will surely be in the domain of deployable and adjustable buildings that shape memory metals will have their biggest impact. Already used to deploy solar panels on spacecraft (box), these actuators could be enlarged to make hinges that open and close shutters automatically in sunlight, that adjust the tension in membranes as required, that automatically open and close ventilation ducts. Larger actuators could store enough power to deploy pantograph-system roofs, with battery-stored heating power or cryogenic fluid cooling power serving only as the trigger mechanism, as in Fuller's seedpod, remote-deployed structures. Or the actuators could be used to fold and deploy canopies and roofs without centralized motors, massive power drives, or bulky gear systems. Architects will no doubt find that shape memory alloys create other marvelous design opportunities.

## Outer Space Materials

Craig Douglas and Depankar Neogi, of the University of Massachusetts at Lowell, have developed a "self-deployable structural element" formed with a core of thermally activated expanding foam heated with a resistance wire (U.S. patent 4,978,564, December 18, 1990). Flattened and rolled up like a paper party blower, the structural member unrolls and becomes round and stiff when an electric current is applied to the heating wire, all without human intervention. The same heating element also cures the outer jacket of the structural member, which is made of a braided carbon-epoxy composite stronger, lighter, and more stable than aluminum. The azodicarbonamide blowing agent Celogen OT, a product of Uniroyal Chemical Company, has the property of decomposing quickly to yield a high volume of gas, causing a sudden increase of pressure in the coiled member at the relatively low temperature of 187 degrees centigrade (369 degrees Fahrenheit). To achieve the maximum coil, only one end of the system is capped until the manufacture of the tube is completed. Such clever attention to detail produced impressive results in prototype tests: tubes uncoiled in twenty seconds (after heating up for about an hour with the application of a modest 65.75 watts per deployed meter). Although the stowed-to-deployed volume ratio is only about 1:2, Neogi and Douglas say that their system offers higher reliability (because of the absence of linkages) at lower costs, at potentially greater strengths than other deployable systems.

Another highly mechanized deployment system for outer space is a concept of A. Wilson and his colleagues at Brigham Young University: spraying composite materials on the inside of inflated spheres. In space, a Kevlar fabric dome 100 feet in diameter—with a volume about fifty times greater than the typical cylindrical space module—can be deployed using a gas canister less than 2 feet in diameter and 6 feet long. Once the structure is deployed, the fabric is coated with 5-inch-thick polyurethane foam and then by a half-inch-thick graphite-epoxy composite; the coating is performed automatically by a spraying machine attached to a telescoping arm inside the rotating sphere. Several concentric spheres could be built this way. Because the cost of shipping materials and deployable structures into space is approximately $4,500 per pound, there is, according to Wilson, an important advantage to deployable systems that can greatly expand their volume after shipping. Inflatable structures made rigid by the sprayed application of durable materials could meet the bill.

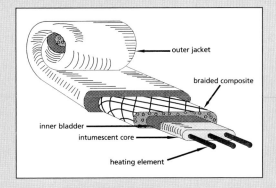

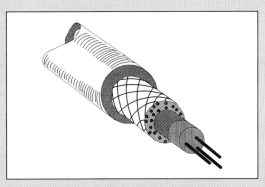

Heat creates gas, which unrolls this structural element for use in deployable structures in space. (Drawings courtesy Craig P. Douglas and Depankar Neogi.)

## Smart Materials

The greatest innovation in materials science is the creation of "smart" materials, designed on biological models. Smart materials are systems that monitor themselves, self-adjust and self-repair, learn to do things the easy way, and know when to quit; they contain strength elements (bones), sensors (nerves), computational networks (brains), and actuators (muscles). Not surprisingly, Craig A. Rogers, of the Center for Intelligent Material Systems and Structures, Virginia Polytechnic Institute, frequently finds himself talking with zoologists. Yet these pseudo-biological systems are localized and automatic, more like knowledgeable rubber bands than error-prone, high-maintenance robots. According to Ken Chong and S. C. Liu, of the National Science Foundation, among the more ambitious uses of smart materials are "aircraft skins embedded with fiber optic sensors to detect structural flaws; bridges with sensing/actuating elements to counter violent vibrations; and stealth submarine vehicles with swimming muscles made of special polymers."[23]

For civil engineering applications, smart materials offer a radical change of practice: designing, not for the "worst-case" scenario, but for the "birth-to-retirement" scenario. *Birth-to-retirement* means using sensors in the manufacturing process to acquire accurate knowledge of the materials used in a structure in order to monitor and, if possible, actively adjust for overloading in the completed structure, automatically repair any small weakness before it threatens the structure as a whole, inform users and occupants of dangerous conditions, and inform owners when it is appropriate to decommission a structure. Bridges could say when they should close temporarily or traffic should be slowed, when their adjustable poststressing actuators were at their limit, and when material fatigue required the building of a new bridge. A ladder could use electricity to stiffen itself or announce when it is overloaded. A space truss, or a tenseg-

rity truss, could control the lengths of its struts to balance loads or warn when it could not. In these smart structures efficiency of design would replace redundancy. Each building would not only be a miracle of visual lightness but would have increased safety and reduced overall costs.[24]

Other uses for smart materials have been imagined. Windows and membranes could change their reflectivity as sun conditions change by calling for an increase in electrical charge to a clear gel between layers. Aircraft wings, propellers, helicopter blades, and—currently—supports for precision antennae and telescope surfaces could automatically change shape for optimum performance, reducing vibration and hence fatigue while increasing efficiency of operation. Strain actuators could counteract weak points in a material (around holes or connections) or monitor and counteract catastrophic metal fatigue. Smart materials could be vibration-control mechanisms that selectively interfere with noise-producing vibrations, alleviating one of the most oppressive qualities of the built environment.

Shape memory alloys are already used as actuators in smart systems, especially nickel-titanium, which can deliver about twice the force of copper-based alloys. Their main disadvantage is that because they are activated by heat and cold, their response time is not as fast as that of other materials. Piezoelectric actuators change shape immediately when voltage is applied. Lead zirconate titanate (PZT) is the most commonly used piezoceramic, with a history of use dating back to the 1950s in such mechanisms as optical tracking devices, speakers, ink-jet printers. The change in shape of piezoelectric actuators can be accurately and quickly controlled, but the strain they can induce is less than one-tenth that of nickel-titanium. Magnetostrictive materials are also being investigated, Terfenol-D for one, which contains the rare earth element terbium; they act like piezoelectric materials except that they change shape in magnetic rather than electric fields. Finally, certain fluids can change vis-cosity, even changing from a liquid to a solid, in the presence of electric fields (electrorheological fluids) or magnetic fields (magnetorheological fluids); they can be used to actively dampen vibration in structures.[25]

Sensing functions are critical to smart materials. Embedded optical fibers communicate the state of their matrix by variations in light transmission properties or, in the case of a break, by the absence of light. Piezoelectric materials produce small electrical charges in response to mechanical stress. Such piezoelectric polymers as polyvinylidene fluoride can be formed in thin skins to become, in effect, paint that senses pressure; and they can be formulated to produce information about the direction of the force. So sensitive is PVDF that sensors made from it can read Braille. Sensing material need not be restricted to a surface; it can be embedded in structural material, providing information about the interior state of the material.

The intelligence of smart materials varies. At one end are reactive concretes containing vials of sealant. No sensing, communication, or computation is required for this system to function; the cracking concrete provides the force, at the location, for the sealant to be released. At the opposite extreme are systems with multiple sensors and external power sources driving a central computer that records a retrievable history of the system and perhaps learns to anticipate problems before they occur. A happy balance is somewhere in the middle; biologists are learning how much thinking, reacting, even learning is done lower down the communication chain, in decentralized and limited processors. Yet a hierarchy of processing can be powerful indeed, and current research on neural networks that make many low-level decisions simultaneously holds great promise for intelligent materials.

"Engineering is changing. We will soon have the opportunity to ask structures during their life how they are feeling, where they hurt, have they been abused recently; or better yet, have them identify the abuser."[26] Such knowing, intimate cooperation between structures and engineers will make the current brute-force methods seem wasteful and barbaric. As with every other materials revolution in history, smart materials will liberate designers of spaces in ways too marvelous to now imagine.

# Construction Versus Architecture

I have always found the concept of iced tea a bit ridiculous: all that energy to boil water to make tea that is going to be drunk chilled. Glass office towers strain common sense for a similar reason: they are heat collectors that have to be kept cool. Prepared coated glass reduces light transmission to a minimum, it is true, but photons will be photons, and the problem of cooling and refreshing a closed glass box remains. For contrast, consider the passive cooling system of the traditional Persian house.

Mehdi Bahadori, working at Pahlavi University in Teheran, catalogued examples of thick walls that absorb heat during the hot desert days and exude warmth during the cold nights, domed rooms with open caps that collect and release hot stuffy air, and high parapets that shade roofs and courtyards from morning and afternoon sun. His most compelling example, however, is the thousand-year-old device of the wind tower. It "resembles a chimney, with one end in the basement of the building and the other end rising from the roof," and has several continuous channels running from its base to openings at the top. The tower catches the wind, forces it down to and through the cool basement, then forces the cooled air into rooms on the upper floors. This natural air conditioning can be enhanced in several clever ways: a fountain in the basement can further cool the air by evaporation, or the tower can be separated from the house to be cooled so that the air can be made to flow a longer distance in the cool earth or over an underground stream, or the tower can be built with progressively smaller passageways to speed up and (hence) cool down the moving air. Even when there is no daytime wind, the tower, which has radiated its heat during the cool night, condenses the warm, still air and forces it down the tower. When there is no nighttime wind, the heat transfer in the tower evacuates the house and draws in fresh air through the windows.[1]

Cooling towers are natural, passive systems, opposed to the self-contradictory high-energy, brute-strength cooling systems used in most buildings today. Iced-tea buildings are Rube Goldberg schemes: needlessly complex, convoluted, indirect, and inefficient structures to provide shelter and a controlled environment. We will become increasingly exasperated with them now that alternatives are available. We know how to build adjustable buildings with rational, passive filtering systems that work without huge, energy-consuming, error-prone machines, each panting and puffing against impossible odds like a nineteenth-century Sisyphus caught in a time warp. Why should every house contain a locomotive like the ones in the Gare Saint-Lazare if the inside-outside, outside-inside transfer can be automatic, accomplished without our attention by self-aware, self-regulating membranes?

We will come to feel uneasy in buildings

that were not erected in a safe, deployable way—the way many now feel uneasy looking at even the best Byzantine embroidery, knowing that many people devoted their lives and eyesight to sew tapestries for the privileged few. We will want to see the evidence, to know at a glance how the building went up, as we often now know at a glance how the forces in a building are handled. All around us we will expect to see tensegrity domes and other buildings in which tension is the salient stabilizing force. We will consider worst-case scenarios silly, wasteful, even unsafe. Hybrid structures, with several structural systems in various states of engagement and reserve, will result in delicate, flexible buildings that reconfigure to changing structural demands. It will be obvious to us that they are buildings like subtle algorithms, in contrast to the buildings like mountains of key-punched cards that brute-force methods produce.

Complaints that membrane structures are not permanent or insulated or cost-effective have been refuted by the hundreds of success stories. Deployable buildings are not only feasible but superior to clumsy buildings erected with scaffolding. These engineering-based design solutions cannot fairly be rejected as impractical. I suspect that resistance to exploration of engineering-based design is based on an association of these structures with a simplicity of architectural image. True membrane roofs have looked awkward when arbitrarily plopped on unsuitable buildings, but no other roof would look better if treated so disrespectfully. But when buildings are designed for them, membranes, with their graceful shapes, have an undeniable, classic beauty. They can also have a contemporary image; color, aperiodicity, multiplicity, variety, and appealing details can be as much a part of membrane engineering as the miracle of long spans. Most important, like Wright's beautiful open-plan architecture, which was based on steel-beam engineering, new materials and technologies can redefine beauty as they redefine architecture.

Engineers could assist in the development of the new aesthetic by articulating the evolving theory of organic engineering: making architecture strong and efficient by modeling it on living structures. The theory gives an organizing principle to today's taste for complexity of geometry and image and keeps the new engineering-based designs from being merely technological innovations or vacuous formalisms.

Granted, an emphasis on engineering in the 1960s may have been a stage in the degeneration of architecture in the 1970s and 1980s into an empty, mechanical mannerism, a now-hackneyed aesthetic of catalogue parts so ubiquitous that it has come to be called just Modern Architecture. Many architects reject Modern Architecture in favor of a designed, "felt" architecture of rich colors, patterns, shapes, and scales. Because Modern Architecture does not always sit comfortably in older built environments, these architects, guided by a sense of proportion and the wealth of existing historical architectural detail, have aspired to integrate new structures into cities. Variety in texture and color has been reintroduced as an antidote to an inhuman minimalism that became part of Modern Architecture as practiced by its less inspired acolytes. Self-reference, humor, shtick, and funk became weapons of a useful iconoclasm.

But these sensible adjustments, these attempts to humanize buildings and integrate them into cities, have come at too great a price. Removing engineering and engineers from the design process has gradually separated architecture from the general technological knowledge of culture. Progress in materials science, geometry, construction methodology, and strategies for strength in design can liberate architecture: architectural science is not at war with architectural art.

Some architects and clients fear—falsely—that drawing closer to engineering technology will limit artistic expression. Far more dangerous to artistic freedom is clinging to an idiom whose time has passed. Like a Victorian architect complaining that the Crystal Palace had no place for statues, a contemporary one can embrace "art" and miss the new consciousness. Nostalgia, whether straight up and sappy or hidden behind an ironic, self-referential gaze, is fine for a half-hour television show watched after a hard work-out at office or gym, but few will want nostalgia to define their experience of the world: nostalgia

is cowardly. We can have instead the beauty of thoughtful, rational design in which efficiency and complexity are fused, the purposeful organic paradigm realized by mechanical and automatic means; we can have structures of 99 percent inspiration and only 1 percent perspiration, spaces as intricate and lucid as computer-graphic representations of higher-dimensional geometries (fig. 9.1), construction that generates architecture as rich as life.

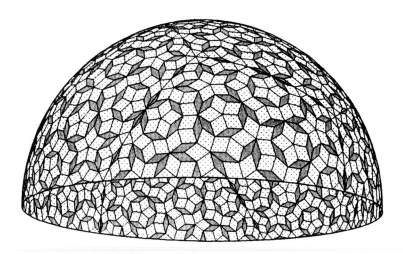

9.1. Haresh Lalvani covers the surface of a sphere with a nonrepeating two-dimensional quasicrystal. (Drawing: Haresh Lalvani and Neil Katz, courtesy Haresh Lalvani.)

# Notes

### Chapter 1: Introduction

1  "A Conversation with Frank Lloyd Wright," NBC television interview by Hugh Downs, released in 1962.

2  Kihlstedt 1984, 132. This view of Paxton prevailed even though by the time the palace was built he was a developer, a director of several railroad companies, and publisher of the *Daily News*, edited by Charles Dickens (Yglesias 1965).

3  Yglesias 1965.

4  Strictly speaking, prestressing occurs only before loading, that is, if the camber was induced by tie rods before the beam was placed in the building. Clearly, however, Paxton understood prestressing as a general concept and was the first to use it in a systematic way.

5  Kihlstedt 1984, 135.

6  Kihlstedt 1984, 140.

7  Berger 1994.

8  Gordon 1978, 95.

9  Brick might be hung 250 feet or "dry stacked on the order of a mile before you would crush the bottom bricks" (David Campbell, personal communication, September 26, 1994). Tension materials are stronger in tension than stiff materials are strong in stiffness; the statement cannot be quantified but is likely to become truer with new developments in material science.

10  French 1988, 62; Campbell, personal communication; Berger, interview, 15 November 1994.

11  Makowski 1993.

12  Salvadori 1980, 65.

### Chapter 2: Membranes

*Japanese Membranes box:* Glaeser 1972; Roland 1970.

1  Dalland 1994.

2  Berger 1976, 1984, 1994. The quotation is from a lecture at the City College of New York in February 1994.

3  Shaeffer 1994, 979.

4  Levy 1991.

5  Geiger 1977, 1986.

6  Campbell et al. 1994, 616.

7  Cost comparisons must be treated cautiously. Costs change greatly from region to region and year to year; and writers are casual about distinctions between cost per foot of coverage and cost per foot of material (which can be vastly different in tensioned membranes), about which parts of the supporting structure are or are not included, about which dollars (past or present) are being counted, and about construction costs as opposed to life-cycle costs.

8  Eekhout 1981.

9  Birdair 1993.

10  Fairweather 1984.

11  Owens-Corning Fiberglass 1981; "Era of Swoops and Billows," 1980; Berger 1984.

12  Berger 1991, 1994. The berm is 60 feet high and was made from eighteen thousand truckloads of dirt. Photographs do not show how steep the seating bowl is or how high the roof is over the seating. This is a big structure.

13  Rebeck & staff 1991; "L'espressività dei particolari," 1993.

14  Berger 1994.

15  Rebeck & staff 1989. In a 35-mile-per-hour wind

in October 1991, the fly cover was ripped beyond repair, and flapping ends damaged several panels in the main membrane. Sound may be problem, too: At certain locations on the perimeter, I heard dishes being cleared away at the center of the structure, and it sounded like an all-out plate fight. Sometimes, too, sound is focused to a peninsula half a mile away, where concerts are given, and sometimes sound is gathered from the peninsula by the membrane. More studies on the acoustical properties of membranes are needed, differentiating between high-frequency sounds, which bounce off membrane, and low-frequency sounds, which seem to pass through. I am concerned, for example, about the potential jet-noise level inside the new Denver airport.

16 "Canada Enters the Dome Age," *Athletics Business*, 1984; Chemfab, 1983.

17 Evans et al. 1993. In general, "roof-first" construction methods are now preferred because they save money, and membranes are well suited to this practice.

18 When photographing the interior one afternoon, I was surprised to have to adjust the aperture as dusk approached. To my eye, the illumination remained constant throughout the afternoon.

19 Berger 1994, 960.

20 Brown 1994, 977.

21 Samyn 1991; *Bâtiment*, 1992.

22 Increased use should eventually bring down the cost of membrane material, so that even small-scale uses are economical. Teflon-coated fiberglass costs about $5.50 a square foot on the roll. Fashioned into a membrane structure and installed, a single layer costs about $15 a square foot (of fabric, not coverage), not including the very substantial cost of the structure that supports the membrane. PVC-coated polyester, such as Samyn used, is generally 20 percent of Teflon-coated fiberglass. Fabrication costs are usually higher, however; the fabric is not as long-lived, and it is not rated for as many uses in the United States as in Europe (see Chapter 8).

## Chapter 3: Tensegrity

*Hanaor on Tensegrity Grids box:* Experts in the field debate arcane definitions of *rigid* and *flexible*. For our purposes, octahedral units of three mutually perpendicular non-intersecting bars, where each bar end is held in place by four

cables, are considered rigid. Units of three bars, where each bar end is held in place by three cables (making a triangular antiprism, with folded rhomb faces), are considered flexible.

It must be emphasized, too, that Hanaor's results refer to his specific tensegrity grids and may not generalize to tensegrity grids of different configurations or even to grids of similar configuration but with different levels of pre-stressing. Still, Hanaor is the only one to have published results of physical model tests to date.

*Engineering by Metaphor box:* Fuller 1983, 179.

1 Motro 1991.

2 Fuller 1962.

3 Lodder 1992, 266, 276; Lodder 1983. "In 1929, Láslo Moholy-Nagy illustrated one of Ioganson's works from the exhibition as a *Study in Balance*, explaining that if the string was pulled, the composition would change to another position and configuration while maintaining its equilibrium" (Lodder 1992, 276).

4 This history comes from Snelson in private communications. In discussing his tensegrity patent, Fuller states that "from 1927 on I sought to discover how to produce what I call tensional integrity structures" (Fuller 1983, 179), and he makes no mention of Snelson, who spent a year in engineering studies and who thought about the general implications of the idea.

5 Fuller 1962, 1.

6 Engineers inspired by Fuller's work have discovered many other tensegrity systems. Oren Vilnay, of Israel's Institute of Technology in Haifa, generalized Fuller's single-layer tensegrity system in the *IASS Bulletin* in 1972 and 1977. Vilnay discovered numerous square tensegrity nets with the sides of the squares extended to bind unit to unit, as opposed to Fuller's pentagonal net. Yet the square nets of Vilnay can also be curved to create a single-layer tensegrity dome. Indeed, his version of the single-layer tensegrity dome simplifies the congestion at node ends and has a cleaner look than Fuller's, although its longer and heavier bars make it vulnerable to buckling. Robert Grip, who developed his ideas in 1978 while working in Fuller's Philadelphia office, has shown that any polyhedron can be made via tensegrity, and thus multilayered tensegrity grids of many types are possible. Grip further shows that there is an interest-

ing relation between tensegrity polyhedra and their duals (in which vertices are truncated and replaced with faces). For example, the dual of a cube is an octahedron: lines joining the centers of the cube's six faces cut off each of the cube's eight corners with a triangle. (In general, dual transformations replace vertices with faces while keeping the number of edges the same.) A Grip tensegrity cube has twelve rods, one on each edge of the cube. The rods converge at the vertices, but they do not quite meet, instead making small triangles of the dual figure, the octahedron. If rods can slide on the cables, the small triangles can grow until they dominate the shape of the faces, making an octahedron with small squares, not points, at the vertices. In my opinion, this interesting insight has not yet been fully exploited. Grip's units are not optimal, however, because they originate from tensegrity units where every edge is a bar instead of a cable (Grip 1992).

7  The patent is reference 1.377.290, dated September 1964, based on a submission of June 1959.

8  Emmerich 1993 ("Spherical Structures").

9  The minimum length of the prism's diagonals is the square root of 2. Both Sergio Pellegrino and Motro have determined that for static equilibrium in triangular antiprisms the ratio of cable length to bar length for antiprismatic structures must be 1:2.25. The ratio of cable length to bar length for other antiprism geometries is given by Motro in the following formula:

$$\frac{s}{c} = \sqrt{\frac{1}{\sin\frac{\pi}{p}} \cdot \left[\sin\left(\theta + \frac{\pi}{p}\right) + \sin\frac{\pi}{p}\right]}$$

where $s$ is the length of the strut, $c$ is the length of the cable, $p$ is the number of edges of the polygon, and $\theta$ is the degree of antiprismatic rotation between the top and bottom polygons (Motro 1990, forthcoming).

10  Motro 1990, 1991. Another way to view this tensegrity grid is to see it as a tessellation of four-sided antiprisms; here, the tensegrity units are tessellated node to node. The antiprisms are also half-cuboctahedra.

11  Motro's tensegrity grid was made to demonstrate that the exact shape of a stable tensegrity system and the degree of prestressing required to realize that shape cannot be predicted with the mathematical tools currently used. It is disappointing to note that geometrically pure

tensegrity units, in which a selection of nodes lie exactly in a plane, may not be mechanically stable in every case. Nor is measuring the exact prestress in an existing tensegrity system an easy task. If tensegrity systems are to be used in unforgiving applications, such as those involving rigid cladding, more theoretical work needs to be done. Motro and his colleagues are working on such form-finding algorithms (Motro, Belkacem & Vassart 1994; Motro forthcoming).

12  Fuller 1983, 201; Fuller 1964.

13  Earlier Robert Le Ricolais invented a flat disk tensegrity roof; Berger's roof is a dome.

14  Robinson 1989; Tuchman & Shin 1986; Campbell, private communication.

15  In a letter of September 26, 1994, Campbell demonstrates how one nontriangulated dome is quite rigid: "The recently complete 120m span Taoyuan Cabledome [in Taiwan] is a good example. The structure has three hoops, 16 radials, with a single focus on a circular span. The structure's behavior is summarized as follows:

"The Taoyuan structure is quite stiff when subjected to uniform loads. For example, the maximum deflection we predict under full uniform wind suction is 235mm (0.83') or 1/474 of the span. Characteristically, the maximum deflection is not at the center but is at the inner hoop; in fact the second and third hoops have nominally the same direction.

"The structure is much more flexible when subjected to non-uniform wind loads. One load condition used in the design of the Taoyuan roof has ½ of the roof loaded with downward pressure and the other ½ loaded with upward pressure. The case analyzed is probably not realistic in its severity, but nonetheless was used in the design and detailing of the roof. The maximum deflection in this case also occurs at the inner hoop: −1,360mm (−4.46') or 1/88 of the span." A further advantage of non-triangulation is that even on non-circular plan domes all the top and bottom nodes can be standard, which greatly reduces the cost of their fabrication.

16  Robinson 1989; Rebeck & Campbell 1990.

17  Geiger 1988 (IASS Bulletin), 1988 (patent).

18  The deflection-to-span ratio is 1:350 (Levy, interview, May 1994).

19  Levy 1991, 1990.

20  Levy, Castro & Jing 1991; Levy & Castro 1991; Levy, Terry & Jing 1992.

## Chapter 4: Deployable Structures

*Outer Space Structures box:* Pellegrino 1991, 1; Miura 1989, 1993. Pellegrino's team also built a mast that was 1.2 meters high when deployed. The erection sequence was repeated twenty-one times; in 90 percent of the cases the uppermost node reached a position within a remarkable 0.5 millimeter radius. The height of the different deployments varied by only 0.3 millimeter, showing a great degree of accuracy. When loaded, this four-unit-high stack of 424-millimeter rods proved to be quite rigid, deflecting only 1 millimeter per kilo of weight. Later prototypes include a mast with a stacked-octahedra configuration (fig.). These prototypes have, in length, a collapsed-to-deployed ratio of 1:10 and exhibit similar or better reliability and accuracy. Finally, the team designed and made a deployable ring. When folded, it measured 0.6 meter, and it fully deploys to a diameter of 3.164 meters, with tension in all cables between 68 and 24 newtons

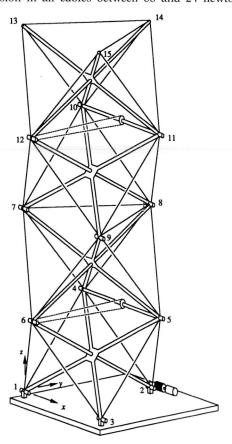

(15.3 to 5.4 pounds of force), insuring a degree of stability to external loads. Ten deployments produced variations of placement of plus or minus 0.3 millimeter, which means that each deployment results in the same structure (Pellegrino & You 1993; Kwan & Pellegrino 1993).

*How to Construct a Tensegrity Dome box:* Levy, Terry & Jing 1992.

1  Marks 1973.
2  Colonel Henry C. Lane, "A Study of Shelter Logistics" (Aviation Logistics Branch, U.S. Marine Corps, 1958), 1, 113.
3  Kirschenbaum, private communication, 1994.
4  Valcárcel, Escrig Pallarés & Martín 1993; Piñero 1965. The patent was granted first in Spain on April 21, 1961,
5  Piñero 1965, n. 15. Between 1976 and 1987, the American inventor T. R. Zeigler received five U.S. patents on similar implementations, including one for a geodesic dome in 1977 (patent 4,026,313).
6  Valcárcel, Escrig Pallarés & Martín 1994, 753; see also Valcárcel, Escrig Pallarés & Martín 1993; Escrig Pallarés & Valcárcel 1993 (*IJSS*).
7  Rosenfeld, Ben-Ami & Logcher 1993. See *IJSS* 8, nos. 1–2 (1993), a special issue on deployable structures edited by Sergio Pellegrino, for a summary of current research.
8  Hanaor 1993 (*IJSS*).
9  Kawaguchi & Abe 1992; Kawaguchi 1994.
10  Kawaguchi & Abe 1992, 76.
11  Kawaguchi & Abe 1992; Kawaguchi 1994. It has not escaped my attention that the hydraulic control room, staffed by the engineer and the architect, as well as by equipment operators, was located underneath the roof as it was raised, showing the confidence that the engineers had in their system.
12  Ninety-one percent of the roof can be retracted in twenty minutes; the system can function in winds of up to 65 miles per hour; and the system has been successfully deployed more than 200 times. Such impressive statistics are balanced by another: the roof costs $262 per square foot, compared with $40 per square foot for the typical inflated membrane roof, in constant 1993 dollars (Allen 1992; Campbell 1994).
13  Saitoh & Kaneda 1992; Saitoh & others 1992; Saitoh, interviews, 1992, 1994.

14  Saitoh & Kaneda 1992; Saitoh, interview, April 20, 1994.

15  Harriman 1991; Dalland 1994.

16  Hernández & Zalewski 1993.

17  Zalewski, in an 1994 interview, noted his regret that the structure is not completely deployable.

## Chapter 5: Shells

*Spanish Shells box:* Collins 1960 (on Gaudí); Billington 1983 (on Candela). See Billington, too, for one of the rare discussions of Candela and Isler in English.

1  Ramm 1991.

2  Isler 1982, 647; Isler, private communication, April 24, 1994. In a rather typical shell 10 centimeters thick with a curvature defined by a 2,000-centimeter radius, the ratio of 10:2,000, or 1:200, is squared in the case of the sphere, giving 1:40,000. But for the cylinder the ratio is cubed, becoming 1:8,000,000—only 0.5 percent of the buckling capacity of the sphere. In specific cases, the exponents are greater than 2 and less than 3, respectively, and other factors in the equation also change. The net result is that cylinders are about 30 times weaker, not 200 times weaker, than spheres.

3  Isler 1982, 672; Isler 1994.

4  Isler 1991, 68; Isler, private communication.

5  Isler 1993, 56.

6  Isler 1993.

7  "For instance, if my concrete shell is loaded with its proper weight of 200kg/m$^2$, I get in every point of the model shell the same stresses as the real when I also load it with 200kg/m$^2$! Our model here has ⅙ of a m$^2$. So I have to load the model with ⅙ of 200 kg = 33 kg" (Isler 1993, 55).

8  Andrés & Ortega 1991, 70; Andrés, Ortega & Schiratti 1994. However, 2 percent is a large deviation compared with the 0.2 percent deviation that Isler says is critical to the stability of his shells (Isler 1993).

9  Ribs add complications other than simply their self-weight: "The shell and the rib have different stiffness, which means that they respond differently to load and thermal change. This produces 'incompatibilities' that produce secondary moments in the shell" (Andrew Vernooy, personal communication, October 19, 1994).

10  Scordelis 1985, 14; Scordelis 1993, 70. In the second reference Scordelis summarizes the state of the art of the computer modeling of shells.

11  Ramm 1991.

12  Maute & Ramm 1994.

13  Billington 1983; Isler 1984.

14  Christiansen, undated; Isler 1984.

15  Isler 1984.

16  Schlaich 1985.

17  Billington 1983.

18  Designers of the building insisted on the particular shapes used, even though they were not good shell shapes, and also insisted that they be real—be self-supporting. As a consequence, the building cost "over twenty times the initial cost estimate for a scaled-down version of the initial plan" (Billington 1983).

## Chapter 6: Hybrids

*Tipis box:* Nabokov & Easton 1989, 24. My conjecture is completely uncorroborated, even disbelieved, by experts.

1  Saitoh 1991; Saitoh & Kaneda 1992.

2  Saitoh & Kaneda 1992.

3  Schlaich & Schober 1994.

4  Schlaich & Schober 1994. Although some engineers might refer to his system of bars and cables as a simple single-layer triangulated grid dome, Schlaich emphasizes the separate qualities of the two parts of the system (reticular dome and cable net), and for good reason. Frei Otto explored and built grid domes before Schlaich, first at Essen in 1962 (his German Building Exhibition Hall); his structure was not secured by a cable net, however.

5  Schlaich & Schober 1994, 14.

6  Kawaguchi & others 1994.

7  Chilton, Choo & Yu 1994, 1071.

8  Chilton, Choo & Coulliette 1994.

9  Gordon 1978.

## Chapter 7: Structural Morphology

*Robert Le Ricolais box:* Emmerich 1994, 8.

*Shapes with Four Dimensions box:* Variations are possible in the arrangement of parts in the 600-cell and especially in the 120-cell polytopes, making a total of sixteen regular polytopes. But generally these small variations are grouped together.

1 The IASS Working Group on Structural Morphology is led by Ture Wester, professor of engineering at Denmark's Royal Academy of Fine Arts, J. François Gabriel, professor of architecture at Syracuse University, Pieter Huybers, professor of engineering at the Delft University of Technology, and René Motro, professor of engineering at the University of Montpellier–II. This core group of four is supported by a trio: Haresh Lalvani, professor of architecture at Pratt Institute; Koji Miyazaki, professor of environmental design at Kyoto University; and myself. Surrounding these seven are a loosely knit band of twenty to forty engineers and architects who make up the working group.

   Structural morphologists should not be confused with structural topologists, although they are good friends. Janos Baracs, professor of engineering at the University of Montreal, has long published the journal *Structural Topology*, where many wonderful ideas have first been publicized. Other morphology study groups are Arthur Loeb's Polymorphs at Harvard's Carpenter Center, the group at Stuttgart's Institute for Lightweight Structures, and the Space Structures group of Hoshyar Nooshin and Zygmut Makowski, of the University of Surrey, who meet once every nine years. An important clearinghouse for all these groups originated in the International Society for the Interdisciplinary Studies of Symmetry, organized by Dénes Nagy and György Darvas in Budapest in 1989.

2 Nooshin, Disney & Yamamoto 1993; Nooshin & Hadker 1993.

3 Oshiro, Yamamoto & Kishimoto 1993.

4 Chu 1993.

5 Huybers 1991, 1993 (*Space Structures 4*), 1993 (*Design Studies*). The icosadodecahedron is most easily visualized as the truncation of an icosahedron by a dodecahedron such that intersecting edges mutually bisect each other. Each of the ten 5-triangle caps is cut away to make a pentagon, leaving twenty remaining tetrahedra.

6 Miyazaki 1990, 1991.

7 Lalvani 1991, 1994. Draw a regular polygon with fourteen sides, for example. Discover the interior angle of the figure. Fourteen divided by two is seven, and there are three integer pairs that total seven: 1 + 6, 2 + 4, 3 + 4. Draw three rhombs, one with the acute angle equal to the interior angle of the fourteen-sided polygon and

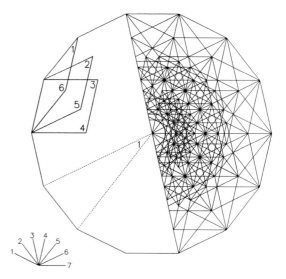

the oblate angle six times that angle, one with the acute angle two times the interior angle and the oblate angle five times that angle, and the last one with the acute angle three times the interior angle and the oblate angle four times the same angle. Combinations of these rhombs will tessellate, filling all of two-dimensional space, and the manner of their tessellation is also specified (there must be fourteen units of the central angle around every point—fourteen 1s or seven 2s, and so forth. These results are proscribed by the fact that the fourteen-sided regular polygon is a symmetrical projection of a seven-dimensional cube (fig.).

8 Pioneers in quasicrystal architecture include the autodidact Steve Baer, who was the first to realize that the nodes of a triacontahedron could be made from standard dodecahedra and that these nodes could be used to make spaceframes with fivefold symmetry. The mathematician Roger Penrose discovered an infinite, aperiodic two-dimensional pattern with fivefold symmetry, although Bernard Kirschenbaum, an artist and architect, preceded him in some respects. Miyazaki first assembled three-dimensional zonohedra into a quasicrystal pattern using dodecahedral nodes. The mathematician John Conway says that he discovered quasicrystals, as does the Japanese physicist Tohru Ogawa. Still others have claims; in fact, my list of people who claim that they invented quasicrystals now contains eleven names. To my mind, however, it

was the Dutch mathematician Nicholas deBruijn who should get the credit. He discovered the algorithm that generates foolproof quasicrystals and that allows computer programs to generate quasicrystals, as I and several others have done. Only by employing such programs is it truly possible to build architectural quasicrystal structures.

9 Ogawa 1985. Fractal subdivisions have a fractal dimension, whereas quasicrystal subdivisions fill space completely.

10 Robbin 1989, 1991, 1992, 1994; Robbin & Reitzel 1993.

11 Gabriel 1991 (*IASS Copenhagen*), 1994.

12 Gabriel 1991 (*IJSS*), 287, 288.

13 Wester's program defines plates as locations on vectors normal to the plate, besides giving information about which plates intersect. This topological approach allows the program greater efficiency and flexibility than a geometric approach in which planes are defined as filling in space between nodes.

14 Baracs 1975, 44.

15 Linkages are ranked as follows: "1) a point is joined to a point by a single edge, 2) a point is joined to a line by two edges, 3) a point is joined to a rigid body by three edges, 4) two skew lines are joined by four edges, 5) a line is joined to a rigid body by five edges, 6) two rigid bodies are joined by six edges" (Baracs 1975, 41).

16 Plate structures with concave corners can be surprising, as the Danish engineer Jørgen Nielsen points out. Pyramid step-up roofs with four steps are stable, but those with five are not. Step-down roofs with three steps are stable, but those with four steps are not. If the steps are not cubic but have rectangular faces, only some rectangular configurations are stable, even though the topology is the same for the stable and unstable configurations (Nielsen 1991). These examples suggest that further theoretical work on plates would be useful.

### Chapter 8: Materials

*Outer Space Materials box:* Neogi & Douglas 1993; Wilson & Aalipour 1993.

1 Gardner 1985; Geiger 1986, 1988 (*IASS Bulletin*).

2 "Landmark Tent," 1994.

3 Birdair reference AP 3656, 11/6/85, p. 12.

4 Gardner 1985; Birdair reference AP 3656.

5 Geiger 1977.

6 Holding a typical sample in my hands, I could stretch it over my thumb, but no matter how I poked and pulled, I could not punch a hole in it or initiate a tear along an edge.

7 Schwitter 1994, 623–24.

8 Stix 1993; Birchall & Kelly 1983.

9 Birchall & Kelly 1983, 105.

10 Stix 1993.

11 Panarese 1992, 47.

12 Panarese 1992, 45.

13 Ghavami & Moreira 1993; Ghavami, *International Journal of Cement Composites and Lightweight Concrete*, forthcoming.

14 Stix 1993.

15 Reitzel 1984, 1992. In the soap bubble example and the Open Cube, the box-within-a-box is also the form of a hypercube projected into three-dimensional space via perspective projection. It would be interesting to study structurally other polytopes projected into the third dimension from the point of view of minimal-surface cell-within-a-cell architectural applications. Baracs (1975) presents a theorem about the instability of projected four-dimensional figures that may refer only to orthogonal projections.

16 Eekhout 1993, 2017.

17 Eekhout 1990.

18 Michalske & Bunker 1987, 122.

19 Michalske & Bunker 1987.

20 Schetky 1979. Nickel-titanium alloy is also called nitinol for NIckel-TItanium, Naval Ordnance Laboratory, where it was invented.

22 Van Moorleghem 1993.

23 Rogers 1992, 1993; Chong & Liu 1992, 5.

24 Rogers 1992.

25 Rogers 1992; Chong & Liu 1992.

26 Rogers 1992, 12.

### Chapter 9: Construction Versus Architecture

1 Bahadori 1978, 144. Bahadori calls the wind-tower cooling system passive because once the tower is built, no further energy is required to cool the building even in the hot summer months. But people who grew up in such houses have told me of doors being constantly opened and shut, of louvered shutters being constantly monitored and adjusted. It might be more accurate, then, to call such buildings "adjustable."

# Select Bibliography

The following sources are used in this bibliography.

**Civil Engineering**    *Civil Engineering,* a monthly journal of the American Society of Civil Engineers (ASCE).

**IASS Atlanta**    *Spatial, Lattice and Tension Structures: Proceedings of the IASS-ASCE International Symposium 1994 (Atlanta),* edited by John F. Abel, John W. Leonard & Celina U. Penalba; published by the American Society of Civil Engineers, 345 East 47th Street, New York, NY 10017-2398.

**IASS Bulletin**    *Bulletin of the International Association for Shell and Space Structures,* published by the IASS, Alfonso XII, 3-28014 Madrid, Spain.

**IASS Copenhagen**    *Spatial Structures at the Turn of the Millennium,* edited by Ture Wester, Stefan J. Medwadowski & Ib Mogensen, the three-volume proceedings of the 1991 IASS symposium in Copenhagen, Denmark; published by the Royal Danish Academy of Fine Arts and distributed by Arkitenten Forlag, Nyhaven 43, DK-1051, Copenhagen K, Denmark.

**IJSS**    *International Journal of Space Structures,* edited by H. Nooshin & Z. S. Makowski, Department of Civil Engineering, University of Surrey; published by Multi-Science Publishing Co., 107 High Street, Brentwood, Essex CM14 4RX, United Kingdom.

**ISISS Budapest**    *Symmetry of Structures,* edited by György Darvas & Dénes Nagy, the two-volume proceedings of the 1989 Budapest symposium of the International Society for Interdisciplinary Studies of Symmetry; published by the Hungarian Academy of Science in Budapest in 1989.

**SMG Newsletter**    *Newsletter of the Structural Morphology Group,* published by its secretariat, Kristen Norgaad, Ramboll, Hannenmann & Hojlund, Bredevej 2, 2830 Virum, Denmark.

**Space Structures 4**    *Space Structures 4,* the two-volume proceedings of the Fourth International Conference on Space Structures, held at the University of Surrey (Guilford, Surrey GU2 5XH, United Kingdom) in September 1993; published by Thomas Telford Services, 1 Heron Quay, London E14 4JD, England, and available in the United States through the American Society of Civil Engineers. A conference is held every nine years.

C. M. Allen, "Toronto Skydome Roof Structure." *IASS Bulletin* 33, no. 110, December 1992.

O. A. Andrés & N. F. Ortega, "Experimental Design of Free Form Shell Roofs." *IASS Copenhagen,* 1991.

O. A. Andrés, N. F. Ortega & G. A. Schiratti, "Comparisons of Two Different Models of a Shell Roof." *IASS Atlanta,* 1994.

Steve Baer, "The Discovery of Space Frames with Five Fold Symmetry." In *Five Fold Symmetry,* ed. Istvan Hargittai. Teaneck, N.J.: World Scientific Publishing, 1991.

———, "Structural System." U.S. Patent Office, no. 3,722,153 (March 27, 1973).

———, *Zome Primer.* Albuquerque: Zomeworks, 1970.

Mehdi N. Bahadori, "Passive Cooling Systems in Iranian Architecture." *Scientific American* 238, no. 2, February 1978.

Thomas Banchoff, *Beyond the Third Dimension.* New York: W. H. Freeman, 1990.

Lawrence C. Bank, "Questioning Composites." *Civil Engineering,* January 1993.

Janos J. Baracs, "Rigidity of Articulated Spatial Panel Structures." *IASS Bulletin* 16, no. 59, December 1975.

*Bâtiment,* no. 227, February 1992. Special issue on Philippe Samyn.

Horst Berger, "Fabric Structures for Public Buildings." *IASS Atlanta,* 1994.

———, "Invitation to a Performance." *Fabrics and Architecture* 3, no. 2, March 1991.

———, "A Decade of Fabric Tension Structures. . . ." *Proceedings of the IASS Symposium on Spatial Roof Structures (Dortmund), 1984.*

———, "Shaping Cable Supported Lightweight Tensile Structures." *IASS Bulletin* 17, no. 63, December 1976.

———, "The Engineering Discipline of Tent Structures." *Architectural Record,* February 1975.

H. Berger & E. M. DePaola, "Tensile Structures Highlight New Denver Airport." *IASS Atlanta,* 1994.

David P. Billington, *The Tower and the Bridge.* New York: Basic Books, 1983.

J. D. Birchall & Anthony Kelly, "New Inorganic Materials." *Scientific American* 248, no. 5, May 1983.

Birdair, Inc., "A 20 Year Case History . . . (La Verne)." Project study. Amherst, N.Y., 1993.

Martin Brown, "Denver International Airport. . . ." *IASS Atlanta,* 1994.

C. R. Calladine, "Buckminster Fuller's 'Tensegrity' Structures and Clerk Maxwell's Rules for the Construction of Stiff Frames." *International Journal for Solids Structures* 14 (1978): 162–72.

David Campbell, "Dream Dome (St. Petersburg)." *Fabrics and Architecture,* Spring 1990.

———, "The Unique Role of Computing. . . ." Suffern, N.Y.: Geiger Engineers, undated.

D. M. Campbell, D. Chen, P. A. Gossen & K. P. Hamilton, "Effects of Spatial Triangulation on the Behavior of 'Tensegrity' Domes." *IASS Atlanta,* 1994.

Chemfab, "Lindsay Park." Project portfolio. 1983.

John Chilton, Ban Seng Choo & Paula Coulliette, "Retractable Roofs Using the Reciprocal Frame." Proceedings of the International Association for Bridge and Structural Engineering conference, Birmingham, U.K., September 1994.

John Chilton, Ban Seng Choo & Olga Popovic, "Morphology of Some Three-Dimensional Beam Grillage Structures. . . ." SFB 230 Conference, Stuttgart, October 1994.

J. C. Chilton, B. S. Choo & L. Yu, "Morphology of Reciprocal Frame Three-Dimensional Grillage Structures." *IASS Atlanta,* 1994.

Ken Chong & Shih-Chi Liu, "Civil Infrastructure Systems Research: Strategic Issues." National Science Foundation, Washington, D.C., 1993.

———, "Engineering Research on Smart Materials." *New Directions* (National Science Foundation publication), vol. 5, no. 5, 1992.

———, STIS, an Electronic Dissemination System of the NSF. Telnet to stis.nsf.gov and log in "public," or e-mail to stisserv@nsf.gov or stiserv@NSF (Bitnet) and request "get stisdirm," or FTP to sis.nsf.gov.

Jack Christiansen, ed., *Hyperbolic Paraboloid Shells: State of the Art.* American Concrete Institute publication Sp 110. Undated.

F. Chu, "SFCAD and Its Applications." *Space Structures 4,* 1993.

George R. Collins, *Antonio Gaudí.* New York: George Braziller, 1960.

H. S. M. Coxeter, *Regular Polytopes.* New York: Dover, 1973.

T. Dalland, "The Body Language of Tensile Structures." *IASS Atlanta,* 1994.

Nicholas deBruijn, "Algebraic Theory of Penrose's Non-Periodic Tilings of the Plane." *Koninklijke Nederlandse Akademie van Wetenschappen. Proceedings,* ser. A, 1981.

Mick Eekhout, "Advanced Glass Space Structures." *Space Structures 4,* 1993.

———, "Glass Space Structures." *IJSS* 5, no. 2, 1990.

———, *Architecture in Space Structures.* Rotterdam: Uitgeverij 010, 1989.

———, "Het 'Dak' Van Munchen." *DeArchitect Thema,* no. 3, May 1981.

D. G. Emmerich, "Robert Le Ricolais." *Le Carré Bleu,* no. 2, 1994.

———, "Absolute Minimal Self-Tensioning Configurations." *Space Structures 4,* 1993.

———, "Composite Polyhedra." *IJSS* 5, nos. 3–4, 1993.

———, "Self-Tensioning Spherical Structures." *IJSS* 5, nos. 3–4, 1993.

———, "Stable Simplex." *Proceedings of the Structural*

*Morphology Seminar*, University of Montpellier–II, 1992.

———, "Symmetrical Stable Simplex." *ISISS Budapest*, 1989.

"The Era of Swoops and Billows." *Progressive Architecture*, June 1980.

F. Escrig Pallarés & J. Valcárcel, "Geometry of Expandable Space Structures." *IJSS* 8, nos. 1–2, 1993.

———, "Modular Space Frame Structures." *Space Structures 4*, 1993.

Ginger S. Evans et al., "The Denver Airport. . . ." *Civil Engineering*, May 1993.

Virginia Fairweather, "Building in Space." *Civil Engineering*, June 1985.

———, "Taj Mahals in the Desert." *Civil Engineering*, November 1984.

M. J. French, *Invention and Evolution Design in Nature and Engineering*. Cambridge: Cambridge University Press, 1988.

R. Buckminster Fuller, *Inventions: The Patented Works of R. Buckminster Fuller*. New York: St. Martin's Press, 1983.

———, "Geodesic Structures." U.S. Patent Office, no. 3,197,927 (August 3, 1965).

———, "Suspension Building." U.S. Patent Office, no. 3,139,957 (July 7, 1964).

———, "Tensegrity." U.S. Patent Office, no. 3,063,521 (November 13, 1962).

J. F. Gabriel, "Space Frames and Polyhedra." *IASS Atlanta*, 1994.

———, "The Architectural Potential of Polyhedra." *Space Structures 4*, 1993.

———, "Megapolyhedra." *IASS Copenhagen*, 1991.

———, "Space Frames: An Alternative to the Architectural Cube." *IJSS* 6, no. 4, 1991.

James B. Gardner, "The Nature of Architectural Fabrics." *Architectural Record*, 1985.

David H. Geiger, "A Cost Comparison of Roof Systems for Sports Halls." *IASS Bulletin* 29, no. 96, April 1988.

———, "Roof Structure." U.S. Patent Office, no. 4,736,553 (April 12, 1988).

———, "The Possibility of Membrane Structures." *IASS Bulletin* 26, no. 91, August 1986.

———, "Developments in Incombustible Fabrics. . . ." *IASS Bulletin* 10, no. 64, August 1977.

David Geiger, Andrew Stefanuk & David Chen, "The Design and Construction of Two Cable Domes for the Korean Olympics." *Proceedings of the IASS Symposium (Osaka), 1986*. Amsterdam: Elsevier Science Publishers, 1986.

K. Ghavami, "Ultimate Load Behavior of Bamboo Reinforced Lightweight Concrete Beams." *International Journal of Cement Composites and Lightweight Concrete*, publication pending.

K. Ghavami & L. E. Moreira, "Double Layer Bamboo Space Structures." *Space Structures 4*, 1993.

K. Ghavami & Z. A. Zielinski, "Permanent Shutter Bamboo Reinforced Concrete Slab." Department of Civil Engineering, Concordia University, February 1988.

Ludwig Glaeser, *The Work of Frei Otto*. New York: Museum of Modern Art, 1972.

J. E. Gordon, *Structures, or Why Things Don't Fall Down*. London: Penguin Books, 1978.

John Gorman, "Pushing the Envelope: Profile of Geiger Engineers." *Fabrics and Architecture* 6, no. 2, March–April 1994.

Robert Grip, ". . . Convex Polyhedra and Tensegrity Systems. . . ." *IJSS* 7, no. 2, 1992.

Stanley Ira Hallet & Rafi Samizay, *Traditional Architecture of Afghanistan*. New York: Garland STPM, 1980.

Kris Hamilton, David Campbell & David Geiger, "Comparison of Air-Supported Roofs on the Vancouver, B.C., and Indianapolis Stadia." *IASS Symposium on Space Structures for Sports Buildings, Beijing*, 1987.

K. P. Hamilton, D. M. Campbell & P. A. Gossen, "Current State of Development and Future Trends in Employment of Air-Supported Roofs in Long-Span Applications." *IASS Atlanta*, 1994.

A. Hanaor, "Developments in Tensegrity Systems: An Overview." *Space Structures 4*, 1993.

———, "Double-Layer Tensegrity Grids as Deployable Structures." *IJSS* 8, nos. 1–2, 1993.

———, "Aspects of Design of Double Layer Tensegrity Domes," *IJSS* 7, no. 2, 1992.

———, "Engineering Properties of Double-Layer Tensegrity Grids." *IASS Copenhagen*, 1991.

Marc Harriman, "Strike Up the Bandstand." *Architecture*, September 1991.

Rodney Heinz, "Plastic Piling." *Civil Engineering*, April 1993.

C. Hernández Merchan & W. Zalewski, "Expandable Structure for the Venezuelan Pavilion at Expo '92." *Space Structures 4*, 1993.

Charles Hoberman, "Radial Expansion/Retraction Truss Structures." U.S. Patent Office, no. 5,024,031 (June 18, 1991).

———, "Reversible Expandable Doubly-Curved Truss Structure." U.S. Patent Office, no. 4,942,700 (July 24, 1990).

P. Huybers, "The Formation of Polyhedra by the Rotation of Polygons." *Space Structures 4,* 1993.

———, "Excursion in Polyhedral Geometry." *IASS Copenhagen,* 1991.

P. Huybers & C. van der Ende, "Prisms and Anti-Prisms." *IASS Atlanta,* 1994.

———, "Computer-Aided Design of Polyhedral Building Structures." *Design Studies* 14, January 1993.

———, "Uniform Polyhedra for Building Structures." *ISISS Budapest,* 1989.

Heinz Isler, "Concrete Shells Today." *IASS Atlanta,* 1994.

———, "Generating Shell Shapes by Physical Experiments." *IASS Bulletin* 34, no. 111, April 1993.

———, "The Quality of Shell Design and Construction." *IASS Bulletin* 32, no. 106, August 1991.

———, "Concrete Shells and Architecture." *IASS Bulletin* 27, no. 91, August 1986.

———, "Aspect of Constructional Physics." *Proceedings of the IASS Symposium on Spatial Roof Structures (Dortmund), 1984.* See also the lecture on formwork.

———, "The Stability of Thin Concrete Shells." *Buckling of Shells,* ed. E. Ramm. Berlin: Springer, 1982.

Jay Kappraff, *Connections: The Geometric Bridge Between Art and Science.* New York: McGraw-Hill, 1991.

Mamoru Kawaguchi, "A Few Attempts in Lattice Dome Structures." *IASS Atlanta,* 1994.

Mamoru Kawaguchi & others, "Structural Tests on the Suspen-Dome System." *IASS Atlanta,* 1994.

Mamoru Kawaguchi & Masaru Abe, "Design and Construction of Sant Jordi Sports Palace." *IASS Bulletin* 33, no. 109, 1992.

Folke T. Kihlstedt, "The Crystal Palace." *Scientific American* 251, no. 4, October 1984.

Yasufumi Kijima, "Image of Structures." *IASS Copenhagen,* 1991.

A. S. K. Kwan & S. Pellegrino, "Design and Performance of the Octahedral Deployable Mast." *Space Structures 4,* 1993.

H. Lalvani, "Hyper-Geodesic Structures: Excerpts from a Visual Catalog." *IASS Atlanta,* 1994.

———, "Morphological Aspects of Space Structures." *Studies in Space Structures,* ed. H. Nooshin. Brentwood, Eng.: Multi-Science Publishing Co., 1991.

———, "Building Structures Based on Polygonal Members and Icosahedral Symmetry." U.S. Patent Office, no. 4,723,382 (February 9, 1988).

———, "Non-Periodic Space Structures." *IJSS* 2, no. 2, 1986.

"A Landmark Tent," *Fabrics and Architecture* 5, no. 7. Spec Guide 1994.

"L'espressività dei particolari." *L'arca,* no. 73, July–August 1993.

Matthys Levy, "The Georgia Dome and Beyond." *IASS Atlanta,* 1994.

———, "Floating Fabric over Georgia Dome." *Civil Engineering,* November 1991.

———, "Hypar-Tensegrity Dome." *Proceedings of the International Symposium on Sports Architecture,* Beijing, November 1990.

Matthys Levy & Gerardo Castro, "Hypar-Tensegrity Dome." *Proceedings of the American Society of Civil Engineers Conference on Automation,* New York, November 1991.

Matthys Levy, Gerardo Castro & Tian Fang Jing, "Hypar-Tensegrity: Optimal Configurations." *IASS Copenhagen,* 1991.

Matthys Levy, Wesley Terry & Tian Fang Jing, "Hypar Tensegrity Dome Construction Methodology." *Proceedings of the IASS-CSCE International Congress 1992 on Innovative Large Span Structures, Toronto, Canada, 1992.*

Christina Lodder, "The Transition to Constructivism." In *The Great Utopia: The Russian and Soviet Avant-Garde, 1915–1932.* Exhib. cat. New York: Guggenheim Museum, 1992.

———, *Russian Constructivism.* New Haven: Yale University Press, 1983.

Z. S. Makowski, "Space Structures—A Review." *Space Structures 4,* 1993.

Robert W. Marks, *The Dymaxion World of Buckminster Fuller.* New York: Anchor Books, 1973.

K. Maute & E. Ramm, "Topology Optimization of Plate and Shell Structures." *IASS Atlanta,* 1994.

"Merchandise Seen in a New Light (Bullock's Store)." *Architectural Record,* February 1982.

Terry A. Michalske & Bruce C. Bunker, "The Fracturing of Glass." *Scientific American* 257, no. 6, December 1987.

Koryo Miura, "Concepts of Deployable Space Structures." *IJSS* 8, nos. 1–2, 1993.

———, "Folding a Plane." *ISISS Budapest,* 1989.

Koji Miyazaki, "Design of Space Structures Derived from Four-Dimensional Regular and Semi-Regular Polytopes." *IASS Copenhagen,* 1991.

———, "Primary Hypergeodesic Polytopes." *IJSS* 5, nos. 3–4, 1990.

———, *An Adventure in Multidimensional Space.* New York: Wiley, 1986.

R. Motro, "Morphology of Tensegrity Systems." *IJSS,* forthcoming.

———, "Form Finding Numerical Methods for Tensegrity Systems." *IASS Atlanta,* 1994.

———, "Morphological Aspects of Spatial Structures Requiring Formfinding Processes." *Space Structures 4,* 1993.

———, "Tensegrity Systems: The State of the Art." *IJSS* 7, no. 2, 1992.

———, "Form of Pre/Self-Stressed Structures." *IASS Copenhagen,* 1991.

———, "Tensegrity Systems and Geodesic Domes." *IJSS* 5, nos. 3–4, 1990.

R. Motro, S. Belkacem & N. Vassart, "Form Finding Numerical Methods for Tensegrity Systems." *IASS Atlanta,* 1994.

Peter Nabokov & Robert Easton, *Native American Architecture.* New York: Oxford University Press, 1989.

D. Neogi & C. D. Douglas, "Development of a Self-Deployable Structural Element for Space Truss Applications." *Space Structures 4,* 1993.

Pier Luigi Nervi, *Structures.* Trans. Giuseppina Salvadori & Mario Salvadori. New York: F. W. Doge Corp., 1956.

Jørgen Nielsen, "Some Stability Problems for Shearwall Structures with Rectangular Plates." *IASS Copenhagen,* 1991.

R. Nijsse, "New Spatial Structures. . . ." *Space Structures 4,* 1993.

H. Nooshin, P. Disney & C. Yamamoto, *Formian.* Brentwood, Eng.: Multi-Science Publishing Co., 1993.

———, "Preprocessing and Postprocessing for Analysis of Space Structures." *IASS Copenhagen,* 1991.

H. Nooshin & D. Hadker, "Exploring Configuration Processing." *Space Structures 4,* 1993.

Tohru Ogawa, "On the Structure of a Quasicrystal." *Journal of the Physics Society of Japan* 45, no. 9 (September 1985), p. 3205.

T. Oshiro, C. Yamamoto & Y. Kishimoto, "An Application of Formex. . . ." *Space Structures 4,* 1993.

Owens-Corning Fiberglass, "Gateway to Mecca." Project report no. 5-FS-10244, January 1981.

William C. Panarese, "Fiber: Good for the Diet?" *Civil Engineering,* May 1992.

Wolf Pearlman, "Structural Topology for Innovative Design in Architecture." *IASS Copenhagen,* 1991.

Charles E. Peck, *A Taxonomy of Fundamental Polyhedra and Tessellations.* Wichita: Charles Peck, 1994.

S. Pellegrino, "A Class of Tensegrity Domes." *IJSS* 7, no. 2, 1992.

———, "Active and Passive Cable Elements in Deployable Masts." *Proceedings of the Forty-second Congress of the International Astronautical Federation,* Montreal, October 1991.

S. Pellegrino & Z. You, "Foldable Ring Structures." *Space Structures 4,* 1993.

Emilio Pérez Piñero, "Three Dimensional Reticular Structure." U.S. Patent Office, no. 3,185,164 (May 25, 1965).

L. Puertas del Rio, "Space Frames for Deployable Domes." *IASS Bulletin* 32, no. 106, August 1991.

Anthony Pugh, *An Introduction to Tensegrity.* Berkeley: University of California Press, 1976.

Ekkehard Ramm, "Shape Finding Method of Shells." *IASS Copenhagen,* 1991.

Ekkehard Ramm & Eberhard Schunck, *Heinz Isler Schalen.* Stuttgart: Karl Kramer, 1989.

Gene Rebeck & staff, "Sound Structures." *Fabrics and Architecture,* March–April 1991.

———, "A Landmark Tent (San Diego)." *Fabrics and Architecture,* Winter 1989.

Gene Rebeck & David Campbell, "Dream Dome." *Fabrics and Architecture,* Spring 1990.

Erik Reitzel, "De la rupture à la structure." Paper presented at the First International Symposium on Engineering and Art, Fondation Vasarely, Aix-en-Provence, 1992.

———, "Le cube overt." *Proceedings of the International Conference on Tall Buildings,* Singapore, 1984.

T. Robbin, "A Quasicrystal for Denmark's COAST." *IASS Atlanta,* 1994.

———, *Fourfield: Computers, Art and the Fourth Dimension.* Boston: Little, Brown, Bullfinch Press, 1992.

———, "Quasicrystal Architecture." *IASS Copenhagen,* 1991.

———, "Quasicrystal Architecture." *ISISS Budapest,* 1989. (Reprinted in *Leonardo* 23, no. 1 (Spring 1990). See also Robbin, "Quasicrystal Architecture." *Proceedings* of SIESA, Groningen, Holland, 1991.)

T. Robbin & E. Reitzel, "A Quasicrystal for Denmark's COAST." *Space Structures 4,* 1993.

Rita Robinson, "Fabric Meets Cable." *Civil Engineering,* February 1989.

Craig A. Rogers, "Rebuilding and Enhancing the Nation's Infrastructure: A Role for Intelligent Material Systems and Structures." National Science Foundation, Washington, D.C., 1993.

———, "Intelligent Material Systems—The Dawn of a New Material Age." Center for Intelligent Material Systems and Structures, Virginia Polytechnic Institute and State University, Blacksburg, Va., 1992.

Conrad Roland, *Frei Otto: Tension Structures.* Trans. C. V. Amerongen. New York: Praeger, 1970.

Y. Rosenfeld, Y. Ben-Ami & R. Logcher, "A Prototype Clicking Scissor-Link Deployable Structure." *IJSS* 8, nos. 1–2, 1993.

Masao Saitoh, "Recent Developments of Hybrid Tension Structures." *IASS Copenhagen,* 1991.

M. Saitoh & others, "Structural Design and Erection of the Izumo Dome." *Proceedings of the IASS-CSCE International Congress 1992 on Innovative Large Span Structures, Toronto, Canada, 1992.*

———, "Design and Construction of the Green Dome Maebashi." *IASS Copenhagen,* 1991.

———, "Experimental Studies on a Long-Span Wooden Dome [Izumo]." *IASS Copenhagen,* 1991.

Masao Saitoh & Katsunori Kaneda, "Design and Construction of Sakata Municipal Gymnasium." *Proceedings of the IASS-CSCE International Congress 1992 on Innovative Large Span Structures, Toronto, Canada, 1992.*

M. Saitoh, A. Okada, K. Maejima & T. Gohda, "Study of . . . Beam String Structure." *IASS Atlanta,* 1994.

M. Saitoh, A. Okada, H. Tabata & T. Mochizuki, "Experimental Study on the Strut Type Cable Net Membrane Structures." *IASS Atlanta,* 1994.

Mario Salvadori, *Why Buildings Stand Up.* New York: Norton, 1980.

Mario Salvadori & Matthys Levy, *Structural Design in*

*Architecture.* 2d ed. Englewood Cliffs, N.J.: Prentice Hall, 1981.

Philippe Samyn, "Steel and Textile Structures: Appropriated Technologies." *IASS Copenhagen,* 1991.

———, "Laboratories in Venafro." Samyn et Associé project report no. 1/222, 1989.

L. McDonald Schetky, "Shape-Memoy Alloys." *Scientific American* 241, no. 5, November 1979.

Jörg Schlaich, "Do Concrete Shells Have a Future?" *IASS Bulletin* 26, no. 89, December 1985.

Jörg Schlaich & Hans Schober, "Glass-Coverd Lightweight Spatial Structures." *IASS Atlanta,* 1994.

C. M. Schwitter, "The Use of ETFE Foils in Lightweight Roof Constructions." *IASS Atlanta,* 1994.

*Scientific American* 255, no. 4, October 1986. Special issue: "Materials for Economic Growth."

Alex C. Scordelis, "Present Status of Nonlinear Analysis in the Design of Concrete Shell Structures." *IASS Bulletin* 34, no. 112, August 1993.

———, "Analysis of Thin Shell Roofs." *IASS Bulletin* 26, no. 87, April 1985.

R. E. Shaeffer, "History and Development of Fabric Structures." *IASS Atlanta,* 1994.

Vladimir V. Shugaev, "Spatial Structures Erected Out of Thin Shell Elements Fabricated on Plane Followed by Bending." *IASS Atlanta,* 1994.

Kenneth Snelson, Letter to René Motro on the development of tensegrity, dated November 27, 1990, for the *IJSS* special issue on tensegrity. Copy to Robbin on September 23, 1991.

———, "Continuous Tension, Discontinuous Compression Structures." U.S. Patent Office, no. 3,169,611 (February 16, 1965).

*Space Structure Mankind, Expo '70.* Osaka: Architectural Association of Japan, 1970.

S. Srivstav & J. F. Abel, "Generalized Computer Modeling of Structures." *IASS Copenhagen,* 1991.

Gary Stix, "Concrete Solutions." *Scientific American* 268, no. 4, April 1993.

W. R. Terry, "Georgia Dome Cable Roof Construction Technique." *IASS Atlanta,* 1994.

Janice L. Tuchman & Shin Ho-Chul, "Olympic Domes First of Their Kind." *Engineering News Record,* March 6, 1986.

J. P. Valcárcel, F. Escrig Pallarés & E. Martín, "Expandable Domes with Incorporated Roofing Elements." *IASS Atlanta,* 1994.

———, "Expandable Domes with Incorporated Roofing Elements." *Space Structures 4*, 1993.

Ole Vanggaard, "Structures Created by Translation." *IASS Copenhagen*, 1991.

W. Van Moorleghem, "The Use of Shape Memory Alloys. . . ." *Space Structures 4*, 1993.

———, "Living Metals." AMT publication. Herk-de-Stad, Belgium, undated.

Oren Vilnay, "Structures Made of Infinite Regular Tensegric Nets." *IASS Bulletin* 18, no. 63, 1977.

Tom Waters, "The Unfolding World of Chuck Hoberman." *Discover*, March 1992.

T. Wester, "The Nature of Structural Morphology." *IASS Atlanta*, 1994.

———, "An Approach to a Form and Force Language Based on Structural Dualism." *IASS Bulletin* 34, no. 113, December 1993.

———, "Efficient Faceted Surface Structures." *Space Structures 4*, 1993.

———, "The Structural Behavior of Arbitrarily Plane-Facetted Spatial Nets." *IASS Copenhagen*, 1991.

———, "Dualistic Symmetry." *ISISS Budapest*, 1989.

———, "The Plate-Lattice Dualism." *IASS Symposium on Space Structures for Sports Buildings, Beijing*, 1987.

———, "Structural Order in Space, Plate Laboratory." Paper presented at the Royal Academy of Fine Arts, Copenhagen, 1984.

Robert A. Wiggs, "The Symmetry of Structure in the Generation of Polyhedral Lattices." *ISISS Budapest*, 1989.

A. Wilson & P. Aalipour, "Thin Shells for Space Stations. . . ." *Space Structures 4*, 1993.

N. Yamada, "Initial Shape Generation for Membrane Structures." *Space Structures 4*, 1993.

Ikuo Yamaguchi et al., "A Study on the Mechanism and Structural Behaviors of Cable Dome." *IASS Symposium on Space Structures for Sports Buildings, Beijing*, 1987.

J. R. C. Yglesias, *London Life and the Great Exhibition of 1851*. London: Longmans, Green, 1965.

Z. You & S. Pellegrino, "Deployable Mesh Reflector." *IASS Atlanta*, 1994.

# Index

Page references to boxes are listed in boldface.